SCANDINAVIAN

COMFORT FOOD

SCANDINAVIAN

TRINE HAHNEMANN

EMBRACING THE ART OF **HYGGE**

COMFORT FOOD

PHOTOGRAPHY BY
COLUMBUS LETH

Hardie Grant

QUADRILLE

CONTENTS

INTRODUCTION

I live a life that revolves around food. I cook, I write, and I own and run a company that cooks and serves lunch for 3,000 people every day in Copenhagen. All my work is based around food – organic and sustainable – and a good life. In a Danish context this always somehow involves hygge – a concept that I describe on page 86.

To describe hygge is difficult because it is so embedded in our culture. It's not cosiness as such; it's a feeling and an expectation, an everyday part of the Danish language. This book is about the way I cook and eat and that will, in turn, inevitably become a story about hygge since it's so ingrained in our food culture. Even the absence of hygge is defined and recognized.

The book is divided into chapters that reflect the way I eat and cook. **What I Eat During the Day** is a range of light recipes for late breakfast and lunch that could easily be turned into dinner. My family's stories and traditions are the focus of **Our Family Meals** – I hope that most people can find time to eat together regularly. I share some of my celebrations with friends and family through the year in **Easter Hygge**, **Friends over for Christmas Lunch** and **Christmas**

Dinner at my House. It is inevitable that I should write about **My Love of Vegetables**, because I enjoy cooking them so much, and I eat a lot of them. In **Soups for Every Season** the recipes are both new and classic. You'll see that I use a lot of vegetables mixed with grains, herbs and spices in **The Salads I Eat**. Finally, as well as vegetables, I could easily live on **The Breads I Bake** and **Something Sweet**.

I am not a fan of food trends that dictate rules about what we should and shouldn't eat; just keeping up with all the rules is stressful. I believe in the importance of food culture, both historically and currently. Eat balanced food, follow the seasons, be responsible, enjoy eating, and make room to indulge now and then. I juice, I eat grains, meat, fish, and lots of cooked and raw vegetables, but I also appreciate cake, and a glass of wine.

Nothing is more vital to me than to have a great time around food with other people. To cook and share: that is our biggest asset in life. I hope this book will inspire you to make life hyggeligt every day, and to cook for friends, strangers, neighbours, lovers and family.

Velbekomme!

WHY I BUY ORGANIC

We all have to eat – that is stating the obvious – but to eat in our modern Western world, we do not have to cook. We have the choice to eat enough calories every day without ever getting near a kitchen. It will surprise no one that I think that is a disaster. Cooking has many functions, and one is making sure that biodiversity is on our plates, which in practice means using a wide range of ingredients over the shifting seasons. Processed foods tend to streamline ingredients so that they get the same process every time. Therefore, you have to eat real cooked food.

I believe very strongly in organic produce, and for one simple reason: I do not want any toxic chemicals in my food. I like to eat clean, tasty, and fair food.

So I try to eat as much organic as possible. All my dairies like milk, cheese, and yogurt are organic; I only bake with organic flour; all eggs and chicken I eat are organic; I only buy organic meat, and the way I can afford that is by only eating meat twice a week. My herbs, I grow myself. All basic vegetables like carrots, onion, garlic, potatoes, and root vegetables are organic. Then I try to buy organic for all the rest as well. Over the last ten years it has become much easier to live organic in Denmark because demand is rising, so supply is growing. Organic has become important business for supermarket growth strategy.

People often complain that organic, certified or not, is more expensive. I say that is not true – not when you understand what goes into growing food. Visit a farm. When did we decide food has to be inexpensive? That decision also comes with a cost, which is our quality of life. The other thing is: also think about eating less, and not wasting food. That will translate directly into your budget. A further idea is to make sure that supermarkets are not driving prices up, so try to buy directly: go to farmers' markets, subscribe to a box scheme wherever you live, and join a co-up or start one in your own community.

I am not a scientist who can explain elaborately, what the problem with non-organic food is. For me it's common sense. Spraying toxic chemicals on our soil and produce, asking farmers to work in that environment, is wrong and at the same time messes with nature's laws, which is asking for disaster. I think toxic chemicals sprayed in nature harm our health; I do not believe you can qualify that statement. Therefore, my dream is that in the next 100 years the world of agriculture will turn organic. I simply do not believe that we can't feed this planet's population on organic food. Mother nature is so clever; we can find that balance. We need to do this wisely, taking all external factors into account.

We have to grow our food in a sustainable way, not waste it. We need to have time to cook and have fun when working in the kitchen. It makes us understand the significance of taste from clean produce, how all these wonderful colourful vegetables that come from the soil can turn into wonderful dishes that make our life enjoyable. It's about having a good life, and I truly believe eating and cooking are a key factor in realizing that!

For a cook it's very simple: you are never better than your produce. This goes for home cooks as well. So, cooking real food also implies that you have to source responsibly. There is a beautiful biological system going on that my farmer friends have explained to me. I love to visit people working in the organic agriculture business and see how their work flourishes. All my knowledge comes from these visits. When I cook, I like to think I support the farmers' hard work.

Growing organic food in a mix of small and large polyface farms is a way to guarantee a better future for our planet. 'Polyface' means that you have both crops and animals and that you grow a diversity of grains, plants, and vegetables. It's like farming in the old days before monoculture factories alienated from nature began to dominate. We do not have to turn back the clock, or start using horses again. It can be done with technology, using all the knowledge we have available today.

I believe as a citizen of this world that we have enormous responsibilities when it comes to how to source the things we eat. We have the power to make changes by taking concise and deliberate decisions when we spend our money on food. I want to spend my money on food grown responsibly, on farms full of life and full of people who work there – farms that allow nature to be part of the daily life that grows there. I would like to be able to pay a visit, go out into the field, and pull up a carrot from the soil without fearing it will kill me when I eat it.

The way we feed ourselves is closely linked to our quality of life. Human culture and organic food should be celebrated at every table in our homes every day.

WHAT I EAT DURING THE DAY

The way we eat has changed enormously over the last couple of decades. We are influenced from all over the globe by the way we travel, or through migration, and most of the world seems to be within our reach when it comes to food. We have in our part of the world become inundated with choices. When I was growing up there were no more than two types of breakfast during the week, and a bit more for weekends. For lunch there was rye bread only, and so forth.

The way people work in each country also defines how our day is organized around meals. In Scandinavia 150 years ago, you ate something hot for lunch, then that changed to rye bread and cold cuts because people no longer went home for their lunch break, staying at the factory instead. So rye bread was the most convenient food for a lunchbox system.

Today, most companies have a canteen where you buy lunch, and that has evolved into a buffet style of eating, often with endless choices of hot or cold food and, if you ask me, too much choice. I like choice, and I like that we can eat different things every day, but it's very important to take the seasons and food waste into account.

I must admit I frequently eat quite irregular meals during the day, because I am often not that hungry in the morning. I like that each day is not the same, that I can have a late breakfast one day, and then at other times I save my appetite for lunch. In this chapter there is a selection of things that I eat where the rules are abandoned. Nowadays I eat when I am hungry. Then, what is most important to me is that I enjoy my meals. I'd rather go hungry than grab something on the go.

BREAKFAST TABLE:
BREAKFAST FOR ME AND MY HUSBAND

I don't eat breakfast every day any more. When my children were school-age, I used to eat breakfast once I had seen them off to school, but now I drink tea, and then I am not really hungry until later – either I have a piece of fruit or wait until lunch. So breakfast at the weekend is something I really look forward to. It is my moment of calm; table set, newspaper ready. I am ready to enjoy my hygge breakfast tea or coffee and perfectly cooked soft-boiled egg. I serve my toasted rye bread with cheese and jam – I was brought up with bread, cheese and jam – then yogurt and fruit compote. Breakfast is all about lingering, and it can take hours to read all the week's newspapers.

SERVES 2

300ml/1¼ cups natural
  yogurt
25g/3 Tbsp jumbo oats
25g/3 Tbsp rye flakes
3 Danish cheeses
Quince-Plum "Jam"
  (see page 184)
Homemade berry jams
  (see page 182)
2 slices of Rye Bread (see
  page 206 for homemade)
4 large eggs

Set the table and make some coffee. Spoon the yogurt into bowls, put the oat and rye flakes into a bowl, place the cheeses on a board, some compote in a bowl and the jams on the table. Toast the rye bread.

Cooking soft-boiled eggs is almost an art-form, and there are so many ways to do it. This is how I do it: place the eggs in a pan of cold water, bring to the boil and then set the timer for 2½ minutes if the eggs have come straight from the fridge, or a little less if they were at room temperature. Serve right away with the rest of the breakfast.

MORNING PORRIDGE

I make porridge from a mixture of flakes that I keep in a jar, with equal amounts of rye, spelt and oat flakes. I grew up always adding salt to my morning porridge.

SERVES 2

125g/4½oz mixed flakes
250ml/1 cup water
100g/3½oz fresh blueberries
1 apple, cored and diced
40g/⅓ cup almonds, chopped
Pinch of salt

To serve (optional)
Raisins
Cold milk

Put the flakes, water, blueberries, apple and almonds in a small saucepan and let them simmer for 8 minutes, stirring frequently, then add the salt and serve right away, with raisins and cold milk if you like.

RYE AND LEMON PORRIDGE

Here is a recipe made with leftovers, using up all your odd slices of rye bread. If you save and store them somewhere they won't go mouldy, after a few weeks you will have enough for rye porridge. This dish has become famous, because Noma and other restaurants have served it for pudding; very delicious. I still really love this sticky, tasty porridge any time of the day. I often had it for breakfast when I was growing up.

SERVES 4

500g/1lb 2oz rye bread,
  preferably stale
1 litre/4 cups water
Juice of ½ lemon and grated
  zest of 1 unwaxed lemon
100ml/scant ½ cup golden
  (corn) syrup
Cold cream or whole milk
  and extra lemon zest,
  to serve

The night before, put the bread into a bowl, cover with the water and leave overnight. The next day, place the contents of the bowl in a saucepan, slowly bring to the boil and let it simmer, whisking, until smooth. Add the lemon juice and let it simmer again, stirring, for 5 minutes, then take off the heat and stir in the lemon zest and syrup. Serve warm with cream or whole milk, and extra lemon zest.

NORDIC BACON AND EGG SANDWICH

If you put bacon and egg together most people will join you and enjoy it, but for me this sandwich also works without bacon, and with tomatoes instead. I would eat this either as a late breakfast or for lunch, especially when I'm working from home or on the weekends.

SERVES 2

6 slices of thick-cut streaky
  bacon
50g/1¾oz kale
1 small garlic clove, chopped
4 very thin slices of rye bread
2 eggs
Sea salt and freshly ground
  black pepper

Fry the bacon until crisp in a frying pan, then remove from the pan. Add the kale and garlic to the pan and sauté in the bacon fat for a few minutes. Remove from the heat and leave in the pan.

Now toast the rye bread and fry the eggs in a separate frying pan.

Place a slice of toasted rye bread on each of 2 plates. Add the kale, then the bacon and finally a fried egg. Sprinkle with salt and pepper and place the second piece of toasted rye bread on top. Serve right away.

RYE PANCAKES WITH BLUEBERRIES AND GOLDEN SYRUP

Pancakes for breakfast are a real treat. I have a bit of an obsession with rye, not only for health reasons but also because I really like the flavour, and it just adds something to so many things. I didn't grow up with American pancakes (they were something you saw in the movies), and never had pancakes in the morning – they were a treat or even dinner. I started making this recipe in the early 1990s when I was living in Washington D.C. and I was very influenced by American cooking.

MAKES ABOUT 14

3 eggs
350ml/scant 1½ cups buttermilk
100ml/scant ½ cup single (light) cream
1 vanilla pod (bean)
150g/1⅓ cups wholegrain stoneground rye flour
150g/1 cup plus 2 Tbsp plain (all-purpose) flour
2 Tbsp sugar
1 tsp baking powder
½ tsp bicarbonate of soda (baking soda)
1½ tsp coarse sea salt
300g/10½oz fresh blueberries
About 75g/⅓ cup butter, for frying
Golden (corn) syrup, to serve

Beat the eggs in a large mixing bowl. Add the buttermilk and cream and beat again. Split the vanilla pod (bean) in half lengthways and scrape out the seeds using the tip of a knife. Mix the vanilla seeds, both flours, sugar, baking powder, bicarbonate of soda (baking soda) and salt together in a bowl, then fold into the egg mixture and beat again to a smooth, thick paste. Stir in two-thirds of the blueberries.

Melt a little of the butter in a frying pan and spoon 3 round pancakes into the pan, about 10cm/4in in diameter. Fry until golden underneath, then gently turn them over and cook until nicely browned on both sides. Repeat with the remaining batter, adding butter to the pan with each batch and keeping the cooked pancakes warm under a tea towel while you make the rest.

Serve right away, with the remaining blueberries and drizzled with syrup.

SLOW JUICES

Juice is refreshing and makes you feel so good when you are feeling tired or just a bit down. That pure shot of vitamins can give you the energy kick you are looking for. I recommend using organic ingredients for juicing.

EACH MAKES ABOUT 700ML/1¼ PINTS (2 SERVINGS)

Root vegetable juice
500g/1lb 2oz beetroot (beets)
500g/1lb 2oz carrots
30g/1oz fresh mint
500g/1lb 2oz dessert apples
100g/3½oz whole unwaxed lemon

Spinach and pineapple
1kg/2lb 3oz pineapple
500g/1lb 2oz spinach
20g/¾oz fresh ginger

Cucumber and tarragon
500g/1lb 2oz pineapple
700g/1lb 9oz cucumber
1 Tbsp fresh tarragon leaves

ROOT VEGETABLE JUICE

Peel the beetroot (beets), and the carrots if not organic. Cut everything into small chunks and press through a slow juicer for a great-tasting, freshly squeezed juice.

SPINACH AND PINEAPPLE JUICE

Peel and core the pineapple, rinse the spinach and peel the ginger. Cut everything into small chunks and press through a slow juicer.

CUCUMBER AND TARRAGON JUICE

Peel and core the pineapple. Chop everything into small chunks and press through a slow juicer for your great, tasty, freshly squeezed juice.

TIP

You can replace the pineapple with apple in the second two recipes, if you prefer.

SMOKED HERRING WITH CREAM CHEESE AND POACHED EGG

Bornholm is an island in the Baltic Sea famous for smoked herring, which is so good fresh from the smokehouse and served with rye bread and raw egg yolk. Just imagine the sun shining, the sea rustling in the background, herring and ice-cold Danish beer: that's your summer hygge.

SERVES 2

2 smoked herring
100g/½ cup cream cheese
2 slices of rye bread
1 handful of crispy green
   salad leaves
¼ cucumber, sliced
2 eggs
6 radishes, chopped
2 Tbsp chopped chives
Sea salt and freshly ground
   black pepper

Rinse the smoked herring and remove all skin and bone then divide into smaller pieces. Spread the cream cheese on the rye bread, arrange the salad leaves over the cream cheese and add the smoked herring then the cucumber on top. Sprinkle over the chopped radish.

Now poach the eggs (see page 25) and place on top of the radishes, sprinkle with chopped chives, and some salt and pepper. Serve right away.

BARLEY FRISÉE SALAD WITH ASPARAGUS AND SPRING ONIONS

A clean and simple salad with a nicely acidic dressing, served with a creamy, sweet poached egg – that for me is the perfect lunch.

SERVES 4

100g/generous ½ cup pearl
   barley (barley)
10 asparagus spears
1 spring onion (scallion)
1 head of frisée salad

For the dressing

2 Tbsp white wine vinegar
1 Tbsp Dijon mustard
1 garlic clove, finely grated
1 tsp shallot, finely chopped
1 tsp honey
3 Tbsp extra virgin olive oil
Sea salt and freshly ground
   black pepper

To serve

4 eggs
Good bread

Cook the pearl barley (barley) in boiling salted water for 20 minutes, then drain and leave to cool. Trim the asparagus spears and cut into 1-cm/½-in pieces. Thinly slice the spring onion (scallion). Mix the salad leaves with the drained pearl barley, asparagus and spring onion in a big bowl.

To make the dressing, whisk the vinegar, mustard, garlic, shallot and honey together, then whisk in the olive oil and season to taste with salt and pepper.

To poach the eggs, crack one at a time into a small cup. Add a dash of vinegar to a pan of steadily simmering water and create a whirlpool in the water using a whisk. Slowly tip one egg into the water, white first. Cook for 3 minutes, then remove with a slotted spoon and place the spoon on kitchen paper to drain excess water. Now poach the remaining eggs, one at a time.

Toss the dressing through the salad and place the poached eggs on top.

TIP

Any leftover chicken will work well in this salad.

DANISH "BURGER" (PARISER BØF)

Despite its name, this has nothing to do with Paris, but is a classic Danish open sandwich, or *smørrebrød*, and is very popular in lunch restaurants. It's often served with an egg, but I like my Pariser bøf with a twist, so serve it with spinach and my apple relish, but it has to have spicy horseradish to give it a punch.

SERVES 2

360g/12½oz minced (ground) beef
200g/7oz spinach
2 Tbsp butter
1 Tbsp capers
2 slices of sourdough or other white bread
Apple Relish (see below)
1 Tbsp finely chopped red onion
2 Tbsp grated fresh horseradish
Sea salt and freshly ground black pepper

For the apple relish

2kg/4lb 6oz apples, unpeeled
200g/1 cup caster (granulated) sugar
100ml/½ cup apple cider vinegar
2 small red chillies
10 cardamom pods
8 cloves
1 cinnamon stick
2 onions, chopped
1 Tbsp mustard seeds

To serve

Cold beer

Form 2 burgers from the minced (ground) beef and sprinkle each side with salt and pepper. Melt 1 Tbsp of the butter in a frying pan and fry the burgers on both sides until medium rare, or more cooked if you like.

Meanwhile, rinse the spinach in cold water several times until clean, then drain well. Melt half the remaining butter and cook the capers for 2–3 minutes. Remove with a slotted spoon and reserve, then add the spinach and let it wilt.

Now melt the remaining butter in a separate frying pan, add the bread and fry on both sides until golden brown. (Alternatively, you can toast the bread in a toaster instead.)

To assemble the open sandwich, place the fried or toasted bread on two plates and arrange the spinach on each. Add a burger to each and top with the Apple Relish, chopped onion, reserved capers and grated horseradish. Sprinkle with pepper and serve right away with the cold beer.

FOR THE APPLE RELISH

Cut the apples into cubes, with the skin on. Put all the ingredients into a saucepan and bring to the boil, then turn down the heat and let it simmer for 30 minutes. Transfer to sterilized jars and store in the refrigerator.

PORK SANDWICH WITH
RED CABBAGE AND HORSERADISH

This is a real leftover sandwich that you especially eat in December, when pork roast is often served, and also over Christmas. My daughter often has her friends over on Boxing Day to eat pork sandwiches and they will also add gravy and a leftover kale salad. They often describe this as the highlight of the Christmas season.

SERVES 2

4 slices of sourdough or
  other bread
1 small handful of crisp salad
4–6 slices of cold roast pork
Leftover crackling, diced

For the red cabbage
100ml/scant ½ cup white
  or apple cider vinegar
50g/⅓ cup caster
  (granulated) sugar
200g/7oz red cabbage

For the horseradish cream
100g/3½oz Greek yogurt
100g/3½oz full-fat crème
  fraîche
½ tsp caster (superfine) sugar
1 Tbsp lime juice
20g/¾oz freshly grated
  horseradish
Sea salt and freshly ground
  black pepper

To prepare the red cabbage, start by whisking the vinegar and sugar together in a bowl until the sugar is dissolved, then thinly slice the red cabbage and add it to the bowl. Let it rest for 30 minutes.

While that is resting, make the horseradish cream. Mix the yogurt and crème fraîche together, then mix in the sugar and lime juice and season with some salt and pepper.

Spread the horseradish cream onto 2 slices of the bread, add some salad and place generous pork slices on top. Drain the red cabbage, season with salt and pepper and place on top of the pork, then add some crackling before topping with the remaining bread slices. Serve right away.

SPINACH AND POTATOES BAKED WITH EGGS

Is it late breakfast, or brunch? I love having people over for breakfast because then we hang out during the day and go for a walk afterwards. Being at friends' houses and eating for hours is how the Danes like to do it! Serve this alongside cheese, jam and some freshly squeezed juice (see page 21).

SERVES 4

500g/1lb 2oz potatoes, unpeeled
2 Tbsp extra virgin olive oil
5 thyme sprigs, leaves only
1kg/2lb 3oz spinach
500g/1lb 2oz brown mushrooms
2 garlic cloves, chopped
1 green chilli, chopped
4 eggs
Sea salt and freshly ground black pepper

To serve
Bread, like the Five-Grain (see page 212 for homemade)

Preheat the oven to 180°C/350°F/gas mark 4.

Rinse the potatoes and cut into small cubes. Heat the olive oil in a frying pan and fry the potatoes with the thyme and some salt for about 10 minutes. Meanwhile, rinse the spinach in cold water several times until clean, then drain well. Steam the spinach and drain well.

Now roughly chop the mushrooms and add them, with the garlic and chilli, to the pan with the potatoes. Sauté for 2 minutes, then take off the heat, mix in the spinach and divide between 4 small ovenproof dishes (or use 2 larger ones). Crack an egg on top of each (or 2 if using 2 dishes), sprinkle with salt and pepper and bake in the oven for about 10 minutes or until the white of the egg is cooked. Serve right away, with bread.

PAN-FRIED BREADED PLAICE WITH PRAWNS AND ASPARAGUS

Smørrebrød (open sandwich) is a really Danish thing as I have described many times in my books. It's a unique food culture and one of our authentic types of fast food. This version is quite fancy and I serve it for lunch, as the main dish. Then I serve cheese and something sweet afterwards. Saturday lunch is big on *smørrebrød*, even if it's just you and your family, or joined by a couple of friends.

SERVES 2

6 asparagus spears
2 eggs
200g/4⅔ cups panko
  breadcrumbs
4 Tbsp plain (all-purpose)
  flour
4 plaice fillets
50–75g/3½–5 Tbsp butter
300g/10½oz cooked peeled
  prawns (shrimp)
Sea salt and freshly ground
  black pepper

For the lemon mayo
1 tsp finely grated unwaxed
  lemon zest and 2 Tbsp
  lemon juice
2 Tbsp Mayonnaise (see page
  120 for homemade)

To serve
2 pieces of rye bread
1 small bunch of chervil
Grated unwaxed lemon zest,
  to decorate

For the lemon mayo, mix the lemon zest and juice into the mayonnaise and set aside in the fridge.

Rinse the asparagus, cut in half and then slice lengthways. Reserve. Beat the eggs in a small bowl, put the breadcrumbs on a plate, mixed with some salt and pepper, and spread the flour out on a separate plate. Dredge a fish fillet through the flour and knock off any excess, then dip it in the beaten egg. Hold it up to drain off any excess egg, then place it in the breadcrumbs. Turn the fish over until evenly coated with a good layer of crumbs, and place on a dish lined with baking parchment. Repeat with the remaining fillets. (You can put the breaded fillets into the fridge at this stage to firm up the breadcrumbs if you wish.)

Now pan-fry the breaded fillets in butter, in batches if necessary, making sure the pan is never dry of butter, for 2–3 minutes on each side until really crisp.

Arrange the bread on 2 plates and place 2 fried fillets on each slice of bread, then 2 slices of lemon, on top of that half the lemon mayo, then the asparagus. Now add the prawns (shrimp) on top, decorate with chervil and lemon zest and sprinkle with salt and pepper to serve.

SNITTER

Snitter makes an easy, informal dinner, for two or a party, and it's a great way to use up leftovers. My *morfar* (grandfather) hated being invited for snitter, because it was often served with tea, which meant he always complained to my *mormor* (grandmother); he did not care for tea. For him, any hygge moment was best with beer.

BEEF AND PICKLES

1 slice of rye bread
10g/2 tsp salted butter
80g/2¾oz sliced cooked beef
Pickled Mixed Vegetables (see page 181)
30g/1oz fried onions (see opposite)

For the horseradish cream
2 Tbsp Greek yogurt
2 tsp freshly grated horseradish
Pinch of sugar
1 tsp lemon juice
Sea salt and freshly ground black pepper

Mix the ingredients for the horseradish cream, adding salt and pepper. Butter the bread, place the beef on top, add horseradish cream and top with pickled vegetables and fried onions.

EGGS AND SMOKED MACKEREL

1 slice of rye bread
10g/2 tsp salted butter
1 egg
½ tsp extra virgin olive oil
75g/2½oz smoked mackerel
2 radishes, thinly sliced
1 tsp chopped thyme
Sea salt and freshly ground black pepper

Butter the rye bread. Beat the egg with some salt and pepper and scramble in a small pan with the olive oil. Place the scrambled egg on the buttered bread, divide the mackerel into 2 pieces and place over the egg. Add the radishes to the top, decorate with thyme and sprinkle with pepper to serve.

PORK AND APPLE SALAD

1 slice of rye bread
10g/2 tsp salted butter
100g/3½oz sliced roast pork
1 tsp chopped thyme
Leftover crackling (optional)

For the apple salad
2 Tbsp finely diced apple
2 tsp finely chopped mint leaves
1 tsp apple cider vinegar
Sea salt and freshly ground black pepper

Butter the rye bread and place the pork on top. Mix the apple salad ingredients together, with salt and pepper to taste, and place on top of the pork. Add the crisp crackling, if you have some, and the thyme, sprinkle with salt and pepper and serve.

CUCUMBER AND GOAT CHEESE CREAM

50g/1¾oz creamy goat cheese
2 Tbsp baby cress, plus extra to decorate
1 slice of rye bread
3 slices of cucumber
Sea salt and freshly ground black pepper

Mix the goat cheese with the baby cress and season with salt and pepper, then spread on the rye bread. Place the slices of cucumber on top and decorate with extra baby cress.

FRIED ONIONS

2 onions
2–3 Tbsp plain (all-purpose) flour
Pinch of salt
500ml/2 cups for deep-frying

Peel the onions and slice into 5-mm/¼-in thick rings. In a bowl, gently mix them with the flour and salt. Transfer to a plate to lose any excess flour. Heat the oil in a deep, heavy-based saucepan until hot enough for an onion ring dropped in to start sizzling right away. Deep-fry the onions in small batches until light golden. Do not cook them for too long, otherwise they will become bitter. Remove from the oil with a slotted spoon, and drain on kitchen paper.

GRILLED CHEESE BEACH SANDWICH

All beaches in Denmark are public, and almost all of our coastline consists of beautiful sandy beaches. The only problem is that the weather is really unpredictable... Summer can be breezy, with temperatures on the low side. But if you are lucky to be there for the few good weeks we do have, it's the best place in world. The sand is not burning hot, the sea is refreshing – not too salty and never too warm – and the daytime temperatures are around 25°C/77°F. And as the sun doesn't go down until 10 at night, you can enjoy long, light days that never seem to end.

SERVES 6–8

16 thick slices of any bread (a little stale is great)
30–50g/2–3½ Tbsp butter
8 slices of Cheddar or Gouda cheese
8 slices of tomato

Butter the bread on both sides and put a cheese and tomato slice between each 2 pieces of bread to make 8 sandwiches. Place in a cast-iron sandwich maker and grill over a fire until crisp and the cheese has melted. Serve with cold beer, sitting next to the fire while the sun sinks low over the horizon.

EASTER HYGGE

Easter is a significant holiday in Scandinavia, but maybe not so much for religious reasons these days. Celebrations and traditions are important, and keeping to traditions throughout the year is a way to define the way we live. We live in a rhythm of change and repetition: change so that we explore new things, repetition to make us feel connected. It's a way of identifying with our story and past. I believe there is something reassuring in repeating certain rituals every year, to celebrate or signify the change in season and light, and Easter heralds the arrival of spring.

In Denmark, Easter is a proper spring holiday, when people often travel to their summerhouse or allotment to start the season. It's common to invite family and friends over for Easter lunch, when we decorate the inside of the house with tree branches, flowers, eggs, small wooden hens and chickens, and on the dining table we set a big bunch of spring branches with Easter eggs hanging from them. After setting the table it's time for lunch, and to spend a long time eating and lingering over the food and, when the weather allows, going for a long walk along the beach.

CURRIED HERRINGS IN BRINE

Curried herrings often come in a sweet mayo dressing, bought in a jar at the supermarket, but I like to prepare my own, and have a range of recipes for making them. Most of them take weeks, but this recipe prepares the herrings the same day that you eat them, making it perfect for a beach house lunch.

SERVES 6

For the brine
500ml/2 cups spirit vinegar (5%)
300g/1⅔ cups caster (granulated) sugar
1 Tbsp black peppercorns
4 cloves
4 cardamom pods
4 bay leaves

For the herrings
100g/1 scant cup stoneground rye flour
4 Tbsp curry powder
12 herring fillets
Butter, for frying
2 apples
2 shallots
Sea salt and freshly ground black pepper

Dill sprig, to decorate
Rye Bread (see page 206 for homemade), to serve

For the brine, add all the ingredients to a pan and bring to the boil. As soon as the sugar has dissolved, take it off the heat off and leave to cool (you can do this the day before).

Mix the rye flour with the curry powder and a pinch each of salt and pepper. Fold the herring fillets lengthways, skin side out, then turn them in the rye flour mixture. Melt a little butter in a frying pan and, working in batches if necessary, fry the herrings for 2–3 minutes on each side. Place all the fried herrings in a deep, wide dish and pour over the cold brine.

Cut the apples into slices and the shallots into rounds, place over the herrings and press them down so the brine covers them. Leave at room temperature for 1–2 hours, then take the herrings out of the brine to a platter. Add the apples and shallots, decorate with pieces of the dill and serve with rye bread.

EASTER LAMB

Celebrating Easter signifies that spring has arrived, and for me, it's the rhythm of the year that is the most important reason for keeping traditions. Traditions give a framework for time as the years go by, and sometimes that can mean abandoning them or throwing them away to allow for change. That is what my parents did in the 60s because we needed the world to profoundly change, especially to allow women to have equal rights and opportunities. Since then, I have been free to create my own traditions and as such, Easter is about eggs for children and people I love – and at least one lunch where lamb is served.

SERVES 6

For the brine
1 leg of lamb, about 3kg/
    6lb 9oz
6 garlic cloves, peeled and
    halved
1 bunch of dill, chopped
2 Tbsp ground coriander
1 green chilli, chopped
1 Tbsp sea salt
Freshly ground black pepper

Preheat the oven to 200°C/400°F/gas mark 6.

Trim the lamb and, using the point of a small, sharp knife, pierce the meat in 12 or so places, cutting 5mm/¼in down into the flesh. Insert a half garlic clove into each incision. Mix the dill, coriander, chilli and salt together, and rub the mixture all over the lamb.

Place the lamb in a large roasting tin and roast for 1 hour 15–1 hour 30 minutes. Check the internal temperature using a thermometer: it should read 62°C/143°F for pink and 70°C/158°F for well done.

Leave to rest for 15 minutes before carving and serving with the salads for Easter lunch.

EASTER POTATO SALAD

If you are lucky, the first new potatoes and asparagus will have arrived from southern Europe in time for Easter, depending on whether it has fallen early or late in the calendar. These are vegetables that tell us that spring is on its way; we always hope that Easter is the turning point for winter. Sometimes it snows at Easter, and other times you can sit outdoors enjoying the sun.

SERVES 6

1kg/2lb 3oz new small
  potatoes, unpeeled
10 asparagus spears
2 spring onions (scallions)
300g/2 cups shelled peas
4 Tbsp chopped mint
4 Tbsp chopped chervil
4 Tbsp extra virgin olive oil
Juice of ½ lemon
Sea salt and freshly ground
  black pepper

Wash the potatoes and cook in boiling, salted water, then drain, leave to cool and cut each one in half. Because asparagus is grown in sandy water, make sure to soak them in water for 10 minutes before using, then trim the asparagus by holding the stalk with one hand at the bottom and bending it a few centimetres away with your other hand to snap off the tougher part. Now slice the asparagus at an angle into 2-cm/¾-in pieces. Thinly slice the spring onions (scallions).

Mix the potatoes, asparagus, spring onions, peas, herbs, oil and lemon juice in a large mixing bowl and fold the salad gently to mix, seasoning to taste with salt and pepper. Place in a serving bowl and serve with the lamb.

CARROT AND CUCUMBER SALAD

A fresh and spicy salad using the first of the season's ramps (wild garlic leaves). If possible, go and pick them yourself in the forest, then they taste even better and fresher.

SERVES 6

2 cucumbers
4 carrots
10 ramp leaves (wild garlic)

For the dressing
8 Tbsp Greek yogurt
3 Tbsp full-fat crème fraîche
3 Tbsp freshly grated
  horseradish
Sea salt and freshly ground
  black pepper

Cut the cucumber into sticks. Peel the carrots and cut into sticks and place both in a mixing bowl. Chop the ramp (wild garlic).

Mix together the dressing ingredients, with salt and pepper to taste, then fold the dressing into the vegetables and chopped ramps. Season to taste with salt and pepper and serve with the lamb and potato salad above.

LEMON MOUSSE (CITRON FROMAGE)

Perfect for spring: light and creamy with an acidic and fresh flavour just as you would experience in the forest in early spring. And, of course, the yellow matches the colour of Easter. This is my husband's absolute favourite pudding, so I do make it often all through the summer, too. This is a Danish classic that he grew up with.

SERVES 6–8

6 sheets of gelatine,
 1.7g each (or 9g in total)
6 eggs, separated
150g/¾ cup caster
 (superfine) sugar
400ml/1½ cups double
 (heavy) cream
150ml/⅔ cup lemon juice
Grated zest of 1 unwaxed
 lemon

To serve

200ml/¾ cup whipping
 cream, whipped
1 Tbsp unwaxed lemon zest,
 julienned

Soak the gelatine in cold water for about 5 minutes. Beat the egg yolks and sugar together with an electric mixer until pale and fluffy. In another clean bowl, whisk the egg whites until fluffy. In a third bowl, whip the cream until light and fluffy.

Drain the gelatine and place in a small pan to melt. When melted, take off the heat and add the lemon juice and zest. Slowly add the lemon and gelatine mixture to the egg yolk mixture, stirring all the time.

Now fold in the egg whites and the whipped cream. Pour into 6 serving glasses and put the rest of the mixture into a big serving bowl for second helpings. Chill in the fridge for a couple of hours or overnight before serving. Serve with the whipped cream and julienned lemon zest on top. The mousse will keep in the fridge for 3–4 days.

EASTER EGGS

Eggs symbolize fertility, health and life, and are therefore perfect as a gesture. And before Easter it's very important to send out letters which have shapes cut out of them and which include a number of dots corresponding to the number of letters in the sender's name. The recipient has to guess who the letter is from and if they don't, they owe the sender an Easter egg.

MAKES 20

300g/10½oz good-quality marzipan (at least 60% almonds)
200g/7oz dark chocolate, finely chopped
30g/1oz walnuts, chopped
1–2 Tbsp finely grated unwaxed lemon zest

Divide the marzipan into 10 small eggs weighing 30g/1oz, and 10 smaller eggs weighing 20g/¾oz, if you like some variation.

To temper the chocolate, melt two-thirds of it in a heatproof bowl set over a pan of barely simmering water, making sure the base of the bowl is not touching the water. As soon as it reaches 50°C/122°F, remove the bowl from the pan and add the remaining chopped chocolate. Mix well until all the chocolate has melted. Gently heat again over the pan of water until it reaches a temperature of 31°C/88°F (it will have dropped below that when you added the chopped chocolate).

Immediately coat the eggs in the tempered chocolate and place on a tray lined with baking parchment. Place the walnuts on some eggs, and the lemon zest on others. Leave the rest plain. Once the chocolate has set, store in an airtight container.

If you like, you can add all kinds of flavourings to the marzipan before you cover it in chocolate, like Cognac, orange zest, nuts or spices. I just happen to like mine simple and classic.

OUR
FAMILY MEALS

I spend a lot of hours in my kitchen; it's an important room in my house, where many things are always going on. There will be a sourdough that needs attention, bread rising, something fermenting, books and magazines to look through. My kitchen is where I work, hang out, drink my morning tea. First and foremost it's where we cook dinner, and we sit and share our meals. Evening meals are rarely skipped in my household.

I step into my kitchen and always clear up a little and take stock while I drink my tea, then I put on my apron, as I hate cooking without one. I then place my big wooden chopping board in the middle of my 16ft-long kitchen table. I get my knives out, a bowl for my vegetable scraps, and a wet cloth for keeping my work station clean. Often I do not know what I am going to cook. I open the refrigerator and see what's hiding, and then I start taking things out and planning what dinner will be like. Then, of course, I sometimes realize I need to write it all down; this could turn out to be a recipe. Lots of times I end up with various stir-fried or steamed vegetables, some boiled rice or grains, and a salad, good bread and olive oil. *Velbekomme*.

LAMB BIX MIX

Biksemad, or *pyt I pande*, is Scandinavian leftover food – it's a fry-up using leftover potatoes and meat. It is often served with a fried egg, sunny-side up. If you don't have any cooked leftovers, use the vegetables you find in your refrigerator: the odd leek, potato and half cabbage you have looked at for a week, wondering how to use them.

SERVES 4

600g/1lb 5oz leftover lamb or other meat
500g/1lb 2oz potatoes, unpeeled
250g/9oz Savoy cabbage
2 Tbsp extra virgin olive oil
2 garlic cloves, chopped
1 green chilli, chopped
2–3 Tbsp Worcestershire sauce
Sea salt and freshly ground black pepper
4 fried eggs, to serve (optional)

Cut the lamb and potatoes into 1.5-cm/½-in cubes, and the cabbage into slices. Heat the oil in a frying pan, add the lamb and brown on all sides, then take out and set aside. Add the potatoes to the same pan and fry over a medium heat for 15 minutes, stirring now and then, and adding a little more oil if needed.

Add the garlic, chilli and cabbage, with some salt and pepper, and mix well, then add back the lamb and sauté for another 5 minutes. Add Worcestershire sauce to taste and serve right away, with or without a fried egg.

MEAT LOAF WITH LINGON SYLT AND SMALL BAKED POTATOES

Traditionally, meat loaf or meatballs were inexpensive food in Scandinavia. In old cookbooks there are recommendations for going to the butcher and asking for well-aged meat and then mincing it by hand, which indicates to me that those meatballs were way more fancy than we think of them today. Meat was not for everyday consumption, so in many ways this is proper old-school cooking; meat should be treasured and not taken for granted, not even minced meat. *Lingon sylt* is a Scandinavian tradition that we eat with both meat and fish. In Sweden people eat *lingon sylt* as often as other nations eat ketchup. As an alternative, you can eat redcurrant jam, but it's not quite the same!

SERVES 4-6

For the meat loaf
200g/7oz brown mushrooms
500g/1lb 2oz minced
  (ground) beef
2 eggs
1 onion, chopped
2 Tbsp thyme leaves,
  chopped
150ml/½ cup whole milk
50g/1 cup breadcrumbs
2 tsp coarse sea salt
100g/3½oz sliced bacon
Freshly ground black pepper

For the potatoes
800g/1lb 14oz small potatoes
1 lemon
3 Tbsp extra virgin olive oil
2 rosemary sprigs
2 garlic cloves, halved
Sea salt and freshly ground
  black pepper

Lingon Sylt (see page 187),
  to serve

Preheat the oven to 180°C/350°F/gas mark 4.

Rinse the potatoes and keep the skin on. Place them in an ovenproof dish. Slice the lemon and add to the dish with the oil, rosemary sprigs, garlic and salt and pepper to taste. Bake in the oven for 45 minutes.

Chop the mushrooms and mix with the minced (ground) beef, eggs, onion, thyme and milk. Now mix in the breadcrumbs, salt and some pepper. Line a roasting tin with baking parchment and form the mixture into 2 loaves. Place them about 5cm/2in apart on the tin, cover with slices of bacon, sprinkle with pepper and bake in the oven for 30–35 minutes. Serve the meatloaf in slices, with the potatoes and some lingon sylt.

I recommend serving this with the Danish Raw Salad (Råkost) on page 160.

MY FAVOURITE WINTER STEW
FROM CHILDHOOD: LABSKOVS

Here is a classic Scandinavian comfort food dish, and probably my favourite: a mash cooked with meat and flavourings, served with chives and pickled beetroot. I always cook enough for two days, because it is even better the second day. This recipe is 100 years old and originally it was made with leftovers. Later, after the Second World War, it became popular in restaurants in Copenhagen, especially in the restaurant in Tivoli Gardens.

SERVES 6

1kg/2lb 3oz chuck steak
50g/3 Tbsp butter
1.2 litres/5 cups water
250g/9oz onions, chopped
6 bay leaves
6 thyme sprigs
4 cloves
1 Tbsp peppercorns, lightly
  crushed
1 Tbsp coarse sea salt
2.5kg/5½ lb floury potatoes

To serve
6 Tbsp chopped chives
Pickled Beetroot
  (see page 178)
Slices of rye bread

Cut the steak into 2-cm/¾-in cubes. Heat 1 Tbsp of the butter in a large saucepan, add the steak and brown lightly, then add the water and bring gradually to the boil, skimming off any froth from the surface. Add the onions, bay leaves, thyme sprigs, cloves, peppercorns and salt and let it simmer for 1 hour.

While it is simmering, peel the potatoes and cut into 2-cm/¾-in cubes. Add to the meat and let it simmer for another hour, or until the meat is very tender and falls apart easily. Drain off any excess water then stir in the remaining 2 Tbsp butter. Use a balloon whisk to mix the potatoes and meat together into a mash, with the stew remaining lumpy. Serve sprinkled with chopped chives, with the pickled beetroot and slices of rye bread alongside it.

ROAST PORK WITH POTATOES AND APPLE RELISH

I think of roast pork as a real treat. It's very important to buy good-quality meat from a pig that has moved around freely and has had a good life and, as that will cost you money, it is for special occasions only. I cook this for small dinner parties, and I love it when people are surprised at how wonderful it tastes. Ask your butcher to score the skin in a harlequin pattern.

SERVES 8

1 lemon
1 whole head of garlic
10 thyme sprigs
3kg/6lb 10oz pork sirloin (free range or organic), bone in and skin scored
10 cloves
4 bay leaves
400ml/1¾ cups water
Flaky sea salt and freshly ground black pepper

For the vegetables
1kg/2lb 3oz medium potatoes, unpeeled
3 onions, unpeeled
4 Tbsp lovage leaves
4 Tbsp parsley leaves

To serve
Apple Relish (see page 26)
Sweet and Sour Cucumber (see page 64)
Brussels Sprouts, Chilli and Oranges (see page 166)

Preheat the oven to 180°C/350°F/gas mark 4.

Slice the lemon and cut the garlic in half. Mix the lemon, garlic and thyme together and place in a roasting tin. Rub the pork with salt and pepper and place on top. Push the cloves and bay leaves into the scored skin incisions and pour half the water into the tin. Roast for 45 minutes.

Meanwhile, wash the potatoes and onion. Halve the potatoes and onion, leaving the skin on. Take the roasting tin out of the oven and place the potatoes and onions around the pork, mixing the fat that has run off the pork into the vegetables. Pour in the remaining water and roast for a further 45–50 minutes. Check the internal temperature. I always use a thermometer, which should read around 62°C/143°F at the thickest point of the roast; continue roasting if it has not reached that temperature. Leave to rest out of the oven for about 15 minutes before carving, keeping the vegetables warm.

Arrange the pork in slices on one big platter, with bones on the side, the crackling on top and the potatoes and onions alongside. Serve with the Apple Relish, Sweet and Sour Cucumber and Brussels Sprouts, Chilli and Oranges. *Velbekomme!*

MORMOR'S YELLOW PEA STEW WITH SALTED PORK BELLY AND PICKLED BEETROOT

I remember eating this stew as a very little girl with my *morfar* (grandfather), but it is a faint memory, so I checked with my mother and she confirmed it. In the 1970s when the big supermarket opened near my *mormor* (grandmother), she liked it for its convenience. They sold this stew in plastic bags, which I never cared for and neither did my mother, but my *mormor* – sadly – thought it was fine, and she never made her stew again. Recently, I asked my mother to find her original recipe and cook it again. It is amazing when made from scratch, even though it takes three days. So here it is. Read the whole recipe and decide on a plan before you start.

SERVES 6–8

For the brine and pork
2 litres/8½ cups water
110g/½ cup fine salt
60g/⅓ cup caster
   (granulated) sugar
1.5kg/3lb 6oz pork belly,
   preferably on the bone

For the stock
200-g/7-oz piece of bacon
2 large, whole onions
1 garlic clove
1 Tbsp black peppercorns
3 bay leaves
10 thyme sprigs
4 litres/4 quarts water

For the soup
500g/2½ cups yellow split
   peas, rinsed
Sea salt and freshly ground
   black pepper

For the vegetables
400g/14oz celeriac
400g/14oz parsley root
300g/10½oz carrots
3 large leeks

Sausages (optional), mustard,
   rye bread, Pickled Beetroot
   (see page 178), to serve

For the brine, boil the water, add the salt and sugar and dissolve. Leave to cool completely. Place the pork belly in a bowl and pour the cold brine over it, making sure the meat is completely covered; use a heavy item to keep it submerged. (Alternatively, you can vacuum pack it.) Cover the bowl with cling film and refrigerate for 2 days.

Take the meat out of the brine and rinse in cold water. Place in a large saucepan with all the stock ingredients, making sure everything is covered with water. Slowly bring to the boil, skim off any froth and let it simmer, covered, for 3 hours. Remove the pork from the stock and set aside. Strain the stock, discarding the aromatics and bacon (which you can slice and serve with the stew later), and use a ladle to skim off as much fat as possible. Measure out 2.5 litres/4½ pints for the soup and transfer to a large, clean saucepan. Add the split peas to the stock, bring to the boil and let it simmer, covered, for at least 1 hour until the peas are quite mushy.

Meanwhile, peel the celeriac and parsley root and cut into small cubes, about 1cm/½in big. Peel and slice the carrots, and slice and rinse the leeks. Cook the celeriac and parsley root in a pan of boiling water for 10 minutes, then add the carrots and leeks and let it boil for another 5 minutes. Drain and set aside, keeping them warm.

Blend the soup using a hand blender until smooth, adding salt and pepper, then pour into a clean pan and heat, stirring. Trim the pork belly of fat and clean off any other residues. Slice the pork – you can either serve it just boiled as it is, or you can fry it in a pan with the sausages, if using. Serve the soup very hot with the drained vegetables, and the sliced pork, sausages, mustard, rye bread and Pickled Beetroot.

PAN-FRIED HERRINGS WITH
NEW POTATOES AND PARSLEY SAUCE

This dish should be eaten in the summer when parsley's flavour is at its strongest. Herring is a super-healthy fish, and there are plenty of them in the sea. I would really love to bring more herrings onto the dinner table of northern-hemisphere homes.

SERVES 4

For the parsley sauce
200g/7oz curly parsley
30g/2 Tbsp salted butter
5 Tbsp plain (all-purpose)
   flour
300ml/1¼ cups boiling water
200ml/¾ cup whole milk
100ml/scant ½ cup double
   (heavy) cream
½ tsp freshly grated nutmeg
Sea salt and freshly ground
   black pepper

For the herrings
100g/1 cup wholegrain
   rye flour
8–12 herring fillets
20–30g/1½–2 Tbsp salted
   butter

To serve
Boiled potatoes
Sweet and Sour Cucumber
   (see page 64)

Start by making the parsley sauce. Rinse the parsley and drain well, then blend it in a food processor until super fine. Now melt the butter in a saucepan, add the flour and whisk to a smooth roux, then add the boiling water a little at a time, whisking after each addition until it has a smooth consistency. Keep going until you have used all the water, then add the milk, cream, nutmeg, parsley and salt and pepper to taste, and stir well. Set aside in the saucepan until needed.

For the herrings, put the rye flour onto a plate and season generously with salt and pepper. Coat the herring fillets in the seasoned flour on their skin sides. Fry in melted butter, in batches if necessary, for 3–4 minutes on each side. Reheat the parsley sauce and serve the herrings and sauce with boiled potatoes, and cucumber salad, if you like.

MORMOR'S BIRTHDAY DINNER OF ROAST CHICKEN, SWEET AND SOUR CUCUMBER AND SEPARATED GRAVY

This is a classic Danish summer dish that is served with variations from region to region. It is my grandmother's recipe, which she always cooked for her birthday, on 16th July. It is very important for all the ingredients to be seasonal, with new potatoes, and it has to be a big, juicy, tasty chicken. I still cook it on my *mormor's* birthday if I am home and not travelling, otherwise I cook it a few times every summer.

SERVES 6

1 large organic chicken
100g/3½oz curly parsley
10 black peppercorns
400ml/1¾ cups water
100ml/½ cup double
   (heavy) cream
Sea salt and freshly ground
   black pepper
1.5kg/3lb 6oz new potatoes,
   to serve

For the sweet and sour cucumber
250ml/1 cup clear vinegar
   (5%)
50ml/¼ cup water
125g/⅔ cup caster
   (granulated) sugar
2 large cucumbers,
   thinly sliced
Pinch of salt

For the green salad
1 summer lettuce, leaves
   separated
100ml/½ cup single
   (light) cream
1 Tbsp sugar
1 tsp sea salt
2–3 Tbsp lemon juice

Preheat the oven to 180°C/350°F/gas mark 4.

Sprinkle the inside of the chicken with salt and pepper and stuff with the parsley and peppercorns. Place in a roasting tin and rub the outside of the chicken with salt. Roast for 20 minutes then add the water to the tin and roast for 1 hour 15 minutes, depending on size, now and then basting the chicken with the fat that has rendered into the tin, to make the skin crisper. Use a meat thermometer to check the inside of a thigh to see if it is done; it should read 75°C/167°F. Remove to a plate or board to rest and keep warm.

While the chicken is roasting, whisk together the vinegar, water and sugar for the sweet and sour cucumber, and when all the sugar has dissolved add the cucumber slices and salt and set aside, folding gently now and then. Boil the new potatoes until tender, then drain.

For the green salad, rinse the lettuce leaves and drain well. Mix the cream, sugar, salt and lemon juice in a bowl and whisk until the sugar has dissolved. Fold the lettuce leaves through the dressing just before serving.

While the chicken is resting, pour the liquid from the roasting tin into a saucepan, add the cream and bring to the boil, then season with salt and pepper. The gravy will tend to separate, but give it a nice whisk and stir it every now and then with a spoon once on the table.

Carve the chicken and serve with the boiled potatoes, sweet and sour cucumber, green salad and gravy.

A world-class meal!

SUMMER FRIKADELLER

Frikadeller, or meatballs, are served in most Scandinavian homes once a week. But this is not a Scandinavian recipe, because all food cultures have some kind of meatball. I love the idea that there are these dishes that connect food cultures around the world, because most food cultures evolve through exchange, such as trade, migration and travel. My recipe has also evolved from my grandmother's recipe and makes a large quantity. Eat any leftovers cold, for example in a sandwich. If you don't eat pork, then use only beef.

SERVES 6-8

For the frikadeller

500g/1lb 2oz minced (ground) beef

500g/1lb 2oz minced (ground) pork

2 onions, finely chopped

4 garlic cloves, grated

2 Tbsp thyme leaves, chopped

2 red chillies, finely chopped

3 eggs

100g/1¾ cups breadcrumbs

50g/6 Tbsp plain (all-purpose) flour

200ml/¾ cup whole milk

1–2 Tbsp extra virgin olive oil

2–3 Tbsp butter

Sea salt and freshly ground black pepper

For the yogurt dressing

400ml/1¾ cups Greek yogurt

2 Tbsp lemon juice

2 Tbsp chopped dill

2 Tbsp chopped mint

2 Tbsp chopped parsley

Classic Potato Salad (see page 163), to serve

To make the frikadeller, mix the minced (ground) meats, onion, garlic, thyme, chillies and eggs together and beat well. Stir in the breadcrumbs and flour and beat again. Lastly, mix in the milk and season with about 2 Tbsp salt and some pepper.

Preheat the oven to 180°C/350°F/gas mark 4.

Use a spoon and one hand to shape the meatball mixture into small, round balls. Heat the olive oil and butter together in a large frying pan, add the meatballs and fry on all sides until golden brown. Transfer to an ovenproof dish and finish cooking in the oven for 10 minutes.

While they are cooking, make the dressing. Mix the yogurt and lemon juice with the herbs and season to taste with salt and pepper. Serve with the frikadeller and the potato salad.

FISHCAKES WITH HERB SAUCE
AND MINT FRIED POTATOES

In Danish, fishcakes are called *fiskefrikadeller*. The mixture for fishcakes is called *fiskefars* and it can be bought ready made at your local fishmonger in Denmark, which is a very normal thing to do. Usually, it will be really good. I do, though, prefer my own mixture. I serve the fishcakes for dinner, then the next day I eat them on rye bread with *asier* (Danish pickles, see page 178), or cucumber.

SERVES 4

For the fishcakes
600g/1lb 5oz pollack fillet
2 spring onions (scallions)
3 eggs, lightly beaten
100ml/scant ½ cup single (light) cream
Juice from ½ lemon and grated zest from 1 whole unwaxed lemon
2 Tbsp finely chopped dill
5 Tbsp plain (all-purpose) flour
30g/2 Tbsp butter
2 Tbsp extra virgin olive oil
Sea salt and freshly ground black pepper
Cucumber salad, to serve

For the mint fried potatoes
800g/1¾lb small potatoes
8 mint sprigs
50g/3½ Tbsp butter

For the herb sauce
200ml/¾ cup Greek yogurt (10% fat)
2 Tbsp capers
4 Tbsp chopped dill
4 Tbsp chopped parsley

For the mint fried potatoes, rinse the potatoes and boil them in a saucepan with 5 sprigs of the mint until the potatoes are done but firm. Drain and keep them warm until you need them later.

Preheat the oven to 180°C/350°F/gas mark 4.

For the fishcakes, finely chop the pollack fillets and spring onions (scallions) with a very sharp knife, or use a food processor to mince them. Place the chopped fish in a bowl with the spring onions, eggs, cream, lemon juice and zest, and herbs and fold gently, then add the flour, 1 tsp each of salt and pepper, and fold again.

Now that the fishcake mixture is ready, melt the butter in a big frying pan and add the olive oil. Form the fishcake mixture into small balls with a spoon and use your hands to help.

Place the fishcakes gently in the melted butter over a medium heat and fry them for about 7–8 minutes on each side. Now put them in a roasting tray and finish them in the oven for about 10 minutes.

Melt the butter for the potatoes in another frying pan, add the boiled potatoes and fry them slowly until they start to turn golden, then fold in the leaves from the remaining sprigs of mint.

For the herb sauce, mix all the ingredients together.

Serve the fishcakes with the fried potatoes, the herb sauce and a cucumber salad.

WHITE OSSO BUCO WITH ELDERFLOWER AND TARRAGON

Elderflower and tarragon are both ingredients that I grew up with; my mother has always grown tarragon in her garden that we use for cooking, vinegar and preserves. And the excitement is always high when the elder bushes start blossoming along the roadsides in Denmark, and then when it's time to pick the flowers to make cordial.

SERVES 4–6

6–8 pieces of veal (or beef) shin (osso bucco)
50g/6 Tbsp plain (all-purpose) flour
2 Tbsp extra virgin olive oil
50g/3½ Tbsp butter
200g/7oz parsley root
2 celery stalks
5 garlic cloves, chopped
2 shallots, chopped
3 bay leaves
500ml/2 cups dry white wine
500ml/2 cups water
200ml/¾ cup elderflower cordial
10 tarragon sprigs
Sea salt and freshly ground black pepper

To serve
Boiled barley, or bread
A green salad

You will need a sauté pan wide enough to hold the shin pieces in one layer.

Spread the flour out on a plate and season generously with salt and pepper, then coat the shin pieces in the seasoned flour. Heat the oil and butter in the sauté pan, add the shin pieces and brown on both sides until golden and crusted.

Meanwhile, cut the parsley root and celery into 1-cm/½-in cubes. Now distribute the garlic, shallots, parsley root, celery and bay leaves evenly over the shin pieces in the pan, sprinkle with salt and pepper and cook for a few minutes, then turn up the heat and add the wine, water, elderflower cordial and tarragon to the pan. Lower the heat, cover and let it simmer for 1½–2 hours, carefully turning the meat over every 30 minutes, until the meat is tender enough to cut with a spoon. Keep an eye on the liquid in the pan, adding more water if it starts to dry out.

Serve with boiled barley or bread, and a green salad.

ONE-POT GARFISH STEW

This is my father's recipe, from our summer holidays on his sailing boat. Cooking in one pot is really suited to a small kitchen with only one burner, and this is an easy and lovely way to cook garfish, which is a speciality in Scandinavia and in season in spring and then again in early autumn. It is very popular, as can be seen from restaurants' menus during these months.

SERVES 4

600g/1lb 5oz new potatoes, washed and sliced

2 spring onions (scallions), sliced

10 small carrots, cut lengthways if large

10 asparagus spears

200g/1⅓ cups shelled peas

6 garfish fillets

A large bunch of dill

300ml/1¼ cups white wine

200ml/¾ cup double (heavy) cream

Sea salt and freshly ground black pepper

Place the sliced potatoes in the bottom of a large saucepan, then layer the spring onions (scallions), carrots and asparagus on top. Add the garfish, sprinkle with salt and pepper, and top with the peas and dill.

Pour over the wine and cream. Bring to the boil then let it simmer, covered, over a low heat for 15–20 minutes. Serve right away, from the saucepan. I recommend accompanying it with a nice a glass of cold white wine.

ROASTED CHICKEN WITH RHUBARB AND TARRAGON

Rhubarb is a vegetable and, furthermore, great with savoury dishes because it is so sour. I break it up with a little sugar, but I really enjoy the sour flavour with the sweet chicken meat. We have a traditional Danish recipe for chicken and rhubarb compote called *kylling Danoise*. In the 1800s it was very fashionable to name dishes after something French.

SERVES 4

1 organic or free-range
   chicken
2 shallots
3 garlic cloves, halved
10 tarragon sprigs
500g/1lb 2oz rhubarb
50g/⅓ cup caster
   (granulated) sugar
Sea salt and freshly ground
   black pepper

To serve
New potatoes
Green salad

Preheat the oven to 200°C/400°F/gas mark 6.

Cut the chicken into 8 pieces, and the shallots into wedges. Put the chicken pieces in an ovenproof dish with the shallot wedges, garlic and tarragon. Sprinkle with salt and pepper and roast in the oven for 30 minutes.

Meanwhile, cut the rhubarb into 2-cm/¾-in chunks and mix with the sugar in a bowl. Take the chicken out of the oven after its 30 minutes of roasting and place the rhubarb around and under the chicken. Put back in the oven and roast for another 20 minutes. Check to see if the chicken is done (test the thickest part of thigh; if the juices run clear it is cooked) and if not roast for 5–10 minutes more. Serve with new potatoes and a green salad.

COD, THE TRADITIONAL WAY

Cod lives in the waters surrounding Scandinavia and has for generations been a favourite fish, used in a lot of traditional dishes. It used to be a lot cheaper but has become expensive, however I love cooking this for friends for Saturday dinner. I set the table and light candles, open a nice bottle of wine and get everything ready, and after a glass of wine I seat everybody then cook the cod and arrange it on a big platter, served at the table – then it's time to share and eat.

SERVES 6

1-kg/2lb-3oz piece of
  tail end cod, skin on
1 celery stalk
3 carrots
A bunch of parsley
1 bay leaf
200ml/¾ cup water
Sea salt and freshly ground
  black pepper

For the butter sauce
200g/14 Tbsp butter
8 Tbsp chopped dill

To serve
1kg/2lb 3oz new potatoes
200g/7oz bacon lardons
50g/1¾oz freshly grated
  horseradish
200g/7oz Pickled Beetroot
  (see page 178)
4 hard-boiled eggs, roughly
  chopped

Preheat the oven to 180°C/350°F/gas mark 4.

Place the cod in an ovenproof dish. Roughly chop the celery and carrots and fill the inside of the cod with them, as well as the parsley and bay leaf. Add the water to the dish, sprinkle the cod with salt and pepper and cook in the oven for 20–30 minutes, depending on the thickness.

While that is in the oven, boil the potatoes until tender, then drain. Pan-fry the bacon until crisp and golden. Place the bacon, grated horseradish, pickled beetroot and chopped egg in small, separate bowls.

Melt the butter for the sauce in a saucepan and, when it starts to brown, add the dill and let it simmer for a few minutes.

Transfer the cod and vegetables to a serving dish and pour over the butter sauce. Serve with the condiments on the side.

MEATBALLS WITH CELERIAC AND APPLES

Meatballs are not only for frying. In Scandinavia, we have a lot of dishes with boiled meatballs, and when you look in old cookbooks, like the 1837 one by Madam Mangor (see page 132), she includes recipes for meatballs in sauce. This classic dish is, I think, one of my ultimate comfort dishes.

SERVES 8

For the meatballs
500g/1lb 2oz minced (ground) pork
1 small onion, finely grated
½ tsp freshly grated nutmeg
2 eggs, lightly beaten
2 Tbsp plain (all-purpose) flour
2 Tbsp breadcrumbs
1 tsp each of sea salt and freshly ground black pepper

For the broth
2 litres/8½ cups water
1 Tbsp sea salt
3 bay leaves
5 thyme sprigs

600g/1lb 5oz celeriac
2 leeks
3 apples
100g/7 Tbsp butter
3 Tbsp plain (all-purpose) flour
200g/1¼ cups spelt grain
Sea salt and freshly ground black pepper
Small bunch of parsley or chervil, chopped, to serve

Mix the minced pork with all the other meatball ingredients. For the broth, pour the water into a saucepan, add the salt and herbs and bring to the boil.

Use a spoon to form the meatball mixture into balls, lower them into the boiling water and let them cook for 10–15 minutes until they rise to the surface, which means they are done. Remove them from the broth with a slotted spoon and set aside. Strain 800ml/3½ cups of the broth into a jug.

Meanwhile, peel the celeriac and cut into 2-cm/¾-in cubes. Slice the leeks and rinse well. Cut the apples into slices 1cm/½in thick.

Melt the butter in a large saucepan. Add the flour and stir well, then add the reserved broth a little at a time, stirring constantly until the sauce is smooth, without any lumps. Add the leeks and celeriac and let it simmer for 20 minutes. Add the meatballs and apples about 5 minutes before the end of cooking, and cook until the meatballs are warmed through.

Meanwhile, rinse the spelt grain in several changes of cold water. Cook in lightly salted water for 15–20 minutes, then drain. Season the meatball sauce to taste with salt and pepper, sprinkle with the parsley or chervil and serve with the spelt.

CHILDHOOD CURRY (SKRAMSGADE RET)

Nobody in my family can remember how this dish originated or who came up with the recipe. We had it once a week all through my childhood, and it's named after the street we finally settled in after years of living in different communes. There is a Danish classic with minced (ground) meat called million beef, so maybe our family elaborated that recipe and mixed in the flavours of the world.

It's easy to make and, although this will serve 8, I recommend making it for 4 and eating it the following day as well, because it tastes even better then.

SERVES 8

200g/7oz beetroot (beet)
200g/7oz carrots
2 Tbsp extra virgin olive oil
3 Tbsp hot Madras curry powder
2 garlic cloves, finely chopped
1 kg/2lb 3oz minced (ground) beef
2 leeks, sliced and rinsed
Sea salt and freshly ground black pepper

To serve
Chopped flat-leaf parsley
Brown or basmati rice
Mango chutney
Natural yogurt

Peel the beetroot (beet) and carrots. Cut the beetroot into small cubes and slice the carrots. Heat the oil in a large sauté pan and add the curry powder and garlic. Sauté for a few minutes, then add the minced (ground) beef and stir well so the beef separates. Let it simmer for 10 minutes, then add the leeks, carrots and beetroot and let it simmer for 5 more minutes.

Season to taste with salt and pepper and scatter some chopped parsley on top. Serve with rice, mango chutney and yogurt.

SALTED CURED BEEF WITH STEAMED VEGETABLES AND HORSERADISH CREAM

Horseradish is our traditional spice. This recipe is a lighter version of a classic recipe, where meat is served in white sauce. The meat is really tasty and very tender, and I think with this lighter cream I am honouring the tradition while also serving something that is more suitable for the way my family eats today.

SERVES 4–6

1 kg/2lb 3oz beef brisket
1 kg/2lb 3oz potatoes
4 turnips
1 summer cabbage
8 summer (baby) carrots
Fresh chervil, chopped,
   to serve

For the brine
2.5 litres/scant 3 quarts water
150g/⅔ cup fine salt
100g/½ cup caster
   (granulated) sugar
3 bay leaves
1 Tbsp black peppercorns

For the stock
3 litres/3 quarts water
2 bay leaves
1 onion
1 Tbsp coarse sea salt
1 Tbsp black peppercorns

For the horseradish cream
200g/7oz Greek yogurt
200g/7oz full-fat crème
   fraîche
30g/1oz freshly grated
   horseradish
2 Tbsp lime juice
1 tsp caster (granulated)
   sugar
Sea salt and freshly ground
   black pepper

Put all the brine ingredients in a large pan, bring to the boil and let it simmer for a few minutes. Remove from the heat, leave to cool, then pour into a bowl. Add the beef to the cold brine, making sure it is completely covered (use a heavy object to keep it submerged) and refrigerate overnight.

The next day, put all the stock ingredients into a big pan. Drain the beef from the brine and add to the stock. Bring to the boil, skimming off any froth from the surface, then reduce to a simmer. Half cover the pan and let it cook gently for 2½ hours, or until the meat falls apart when tested with a fork. Keep the stock.

While it is cooking, make the horseradish cream. Mix the yogurt and crème fraîche together, then mix in the grated horseradish. Add the lime juice and sugar and stir to mix, then season to taste with salt and pepper.

Rinse the potatoes, turnips, cabbage and carrots. Cut the turnips and cabbage into wedges, and the carrots in half lengthways. Towards the end of the beef cooking time, cook the potatoes in boiling water, then drain. Just before the meat is ready, add the other vegetables to a separate pan, half-cover with some of the reserved beef stock and let it simmer for about 5 minutes. Serve the beef, vegetables and potatoes sprinkled with chervil, with a dollop of horseradish cream on top.

DUCK LEGS WITH POTATOES, APPLES AND BROWN CABBAGE

This recipe feels a little bit like going to some of the wonderful small museums you'll find around Scandinavia, housing paintings by the old masters. It's difficult to explain, but when I eat this dish I can see the landscape in those paintings, the potatoes that come from the soil, the apples that grow on the trees, the ducks walking around in the villages, and the dark kitchens always smelling of cabbage. It is a little bit like time travel.

SERVES 4

5 cardamom pods
1 Tbsp whole allspice berries
4 cloves
1 Tbsp coarse sea salt
4 duck legs
2 tsp freshly ground
  black pepper

For the vegetables
700g/1lb 9oz potatoes,
  unpeeled
4 apples
1 quantity Brown Cabbage
  (see page 110)

Grind the spices to a coarse mixture using a pestle and mortar. Mix in the salt, rub the mixture into the duck legs and refrigerate for 1 hour.

Preheat the oven to 200°C/400°F/gas mark 6.

Place the duck legs in a roasting tin and roast for 1 hour, now and then basting the duck with the fat rendering into the tin as they cook. While they are cooking, cut the potatoes and apples into wedges.

Add potatoes to the tin and roast for another 45 minutes, then add the apples, mix well with the juices in the roasting tin and roast for another 15 minutes. Check that the duck meat is tender and, if not, continue to cook a little longer. Serve with brown cabbage.

THE ART OF HYGGE

Hygge has over recent years spread beyond the Danish borders. It is often described as an idea, or concept, and in a way that is too limited. Hygge is much more than that. It is embedded in our culture in a very profound way, and where that is most evident is in the language. We use the words hygge and hyggelig all the time. All echelons of society use them, but not all activities are hyggelig. Hygge is for everybody.

Our home is our castle. We refer to homes as stylish, or pristine, but the biggest compliment you can give a Dane for their home is that it is hyggeligt. The interior is crucial. The home creates the first frame for hygge – a dining table is important for lingering over dinner. A hyggelig home is a home that feels lived in; a home that reflects who you are and tells your story.

Our homes are very open to spontaneous visits and the first thing you do is offer guests coffee, or sometimes a glass of wine if it's around dinnertime. You'll most likely offer something to eat, too, which just a few decades back would have been a piece of cake, or Danish butter cookies. Alcohol does not have to be part of it.

Hygge is more than anything the atmosphere created by hanging out. We love to hang out at each other's houses for hours and eat, relax, eat again, talk – and it's often fine to tune in and out of what is going on, like looking through the newspaper, or watching a football game in the background. It can go on for hours. NO rules. The only rule is that it has to feel good; it has to be hyggeligt.

Hygge is, therefore, not defined by the place, but by what atmosphere the place has got to offer, together with the companionship and situation. Outside your home, hygge could be at a café, going for a walk, a casual meeting, eating at a restaurant. A long, formal dinner with high-end service would never be described as hyggelig, but if the evening kind of loosens up, the conversation becomes lively, and the ambience makes people get an authentic feeling of being together, then the guests would say that it turned out to be a hyggelig evening after all.

Hygge is often imagined as a winter thing. That is partly true, but hygge is not defined by winter even though we do have a lot of candles at home that we light every evening. I get up in the morning when it is still dark, go down to my kitchen, light the candles, and put the kettle on – then my morning begins.

From the outside, Christmas is properly regarded as the ultimate hygge time. We celebrate for a whole month, decorate our house, meet for Advent on Sundays to bake, make Christmas gifts, collect the Christmas tree in the woods and spend time with family and friends, enjoying traditional cakes, glühwein, and lots of other things that contribute to the ultimate hygge.

But hygge is part of every season. Going to your beach or summerhouse is also all about hygge. The summerhouse often has a fireplace, is full of candles inside and outside; the whole interior is often about hygge; and indoor chairs and outside benches full of pillows and blankets ensure there's room for lots of hygge. Sitting outside in the long and bright Nordic evenings, lingering over dinner, drinking wine and talking into the early hours with friends is quintessential summer hygge. Eating outside on balconies, in parks and gardens, or at the beach is the Danes' favourite thing.

Another important occasion for hygge is birthdays, when we have a tradition of being woken up in bed with a birthday song, then before we go to school or work there will be a breakfast table, as we call it, with gifts.

Hygge at work might sound odd, but Danes try to achieve it by having special breaks, like eating breakfast with their team, which is common once a week in many Danes' working lives. Cake at the office can be a weekly thing for any occasion: that it's Thursday; it's raining; we deserve it. Then several colleagues will take a break for 30 minutes in the afternoon, clear somebody's desk, put

flowers on there, light a candle and get together to enjoy cake and coffee.

Hygge alone is also possible. Again, the language is important. You will say: I'm just going to you stay in and hygge by myself, then you will light a candle, make a cup of tea, see a movie or read a book. You would describe hygge but more importantly, you would feel it.

The opposite of hygge is uhygge, which is scary and profoundly unpleasant. Thrillers are described as uhyggelig in Danish, but it is in a deeper sense than scary. It also describes the atmosphere and the whole feeling of suspense. Scary and unpleasant episodes in life can also be uhyggelig.

To incorporate hygge into your life is to get the best out of it in the sense of generating a relaxed and intimate atmosphere in most of what you do. Cooking does play an important part in that, because there is a lot of love in the gesture of cooking for other people. Eating makes us feel good, and eating with other people makes us feel even better. One way I show my love for life and people is by cooking, so for me hygge and cooking are utterly entwined. When I cook, I start by creating hygge around me, even before the actual meal is going to be enjoyed. So for me, hygge is about getting the best out of our daily life, because life is every day – whatever we are up to.

MY LOVE OF VEGETABLES

For me, cooking is all about vegetables, fruit, berries and herbs; they are the most exciting things about it. I am not vegetarian – I like meat – and I really dislike the word vegetarian, which is a western idea of eating. I think it's wrong to single out food just because it does not contain meat: food is food! So I don't make a distinction in my kitchen, I just cook what I feel like eating, and often that will be meals cooked with vegetables only. I don't call my family to the table by saying "Vegetarian dinner is served". I say, "Dinner is served"!

Vegetables, spices and herbs are where all the flavours are, and where variation is found. It's where endless possibilities exist for combining new dishes. Vegetables also mean seasonal and so eating through the year can be pure excitement. Let's start with early September in Denmark. There is an abundance of everything from corn, pumpkin, mushrooms, root vegetables, cabbage, onions, apples, pears and plums. Then you move into autumn and winter, and cabbage and root vegetables become your staples; you have to use your imagination to make these vegetables exciting every day. And then just when you think you will never eat another celeriac in your life, spring arrives and you have asparagus, ramsons (wild garlic, or ramps), morels, rhubarb and peas. Summer comes with new potatoes, new cabbage and fresh small juicy root vegetables that taste completely different, then radishes, tomatoes and cucumber. Then it all starts over again in this wonderful rhythm of biodiversity that planet earth has created for us to enjoy.

MORELS ON TOAST

The morel season is so short that I just think we should get to eat them once or twice every spring. They have an earthy, nutty flavour and, if you close your eyes, you can let the flavour transport you out into the hardwood forest and connect you to nature, inviting you to run through the spring leafing and damp soil, then let go of winter and experience how all new life is sprouting.

SERVES 2

400g/14oz morels
25g/scant 2 Tbsp butter
2 garlic cloves, chopped
50ml/3½ Tbsp port
100ml/½ cup double
  (heavy) cream
Sea salt and freshly ground
  black pepper

To serve
2 slices of sourdough bread,
  toasted
Handful of chervil

Inspect the morels for dirt and debris, cleaning them off with a dry pastry brush. Trim them and cut each in half, then sauté in the butter with the garlic for about 5 minutes or until they start colouring.

Add the port and let it simmer for a little, then add the cream and let it simmer again for a few minutes. Season to taste with salt and pepper. Serve right away on toasted sourdough and sprinkled with chervil.

ROOT VEGETABLE STEW

Cooking can't be rushed, but that doesn't mean that fast-cooked meals are not delicious. Easy home cooking is necessary in a busy life, so when I am pressed for time and need a quick and rewarding dinner, I turn to this root vegetable stew. In winter I keep my fridge full of root vegetables; they store well and there are endless ways of cooking them. Instead of a main course, this is also great as a side dish served with chicken or cold meats.

SERVES 4

200g/7oz beetroot (beet)
200g/7oz scorzonera
200g/7oz celeriac
200g/7oz carrots
2 Tbsp extra virgin olive oil
1 onion, chopped
3 garlic cloves, chopped
2 Tbsp Madras curry powder
1 Tbsp plain (all-purpose)
  flour
400ml/1¾ cups water
100ml/½ cup double
  (heavy) cream
Juice of ½ lime
Sea salt and freshly ground
  black pepper

To serve
Chopped parsley
Lime wedges
Boiled rice or grains

Peel all the root vegetables and cut into equal-sized chunks, about 1.5cm/½in. Heat the oil in a big saucepan, add the onion, garlic and curry powder and sauté for a few minutes, then add the beetroot (beet) and stir in the flour. Add a quarter of the water and let it simmer for 5 minutes, then add all the remaining vegetables with salt and pepper to taste, and mix well.

Add the remaining water and let it simmer for 10 minutes until the vegetables are al dente, then stir in the cream and lime juice, mixing well. Taste for seasoning and serve sprinkled with parsley and a squeeze of lime juice, with rice or boiled grains.

BEETROOT PATTIES WITH HORSERADISH CREAM

A real classic, beetroot (beet) patties are some of the first vegetarian dishes I remember as a child in the 1970s. Vegetable patties are cheap and delicious at the same time. I don't really like the term "vegetarian food", because why should food be renamed just because there is no meat involved? All across the globe different cultures serve meals from just grains and vegetables and they do not call them anything special; for them it is simply food.

SERVES 6

500g/1lb 2oz beetroot (beet)
1 shallot
50g/⅓ cup sesame seeds
3 eggs, lightly beaten
2–3 Tbsp extra virgin olive oil
Sea salt and freshly ground
   black pepper

For the horseradish cream

200g/1 cup Greek yogurt
200g/¾ cup full-fat crème
   fraîche
30g/1oz fresh, peeled
   horseradish
1 tsp caster (granulated)
   sugar
2 Tbsp lime juice

Peel and grate the beetroot (beet) and peel and finely grate the shallot. In a bowl, mix the grated beetroot and shallot with the sesame seeds and eggs, adding salt and pepper to taste.

Preheat the oven to 180°C/350°F/gas mark 4.

Heat the oil in a frying pan and place spoonfuls of the patty mixture in the pan and cook, without squeezing them so the texture stays quite loose, until golden on both sides. If the mixture seems too loose and irritating to handle, you can add 2 Tbsp plain (all-purpose) flour to the mixture. Transfer the patties to an ovenproof dish and finish cooking in the oven for 10 minutes.

While they are in the oven, make the horseradish cream. Mix the yogurt and crème fraîche together, then grate in the horseradish and mix. Add the sugar and lime juice, season with salt and pepper and serve with the patties.

TIP
These patties can be made with any kind of root vegetable.

ASPARAGUS TARTLETS

Tarteletter are rarely homemade, as most people buy them, or if they bake them themselves, they buy the puff pastry. My friend Louise was coming over for dinner, and I asked her what she would like me to cook for her. She answered: *tarteletter*. So I made the puff pastry and the filling and everything. Louise ate them and was blown away because she had never had homemade *tarteletter* before. I think she used to like her ready-made ones from the supermarket, so in a way I have ruined that: now she knows what homemade tastes like...

SERVES 4

1 quantity Classic Puff Pastry
   (see below), or 500g/1lb 2oz
   ready made
1 egg, lightly beaten
4–6 crisp Romaine salad
   leaves, to serve

For the filling
300g/10½oz asparagus
   spears
1 tsp butter
1 small shallot, finely
   chopped
100ml/½ cup dry white wine
200g/7oz shelled peas
100ml/½ cup double
   (heavy) cream
1 bunch of chervil,
   finely chopped
Sea salt and freshly ground
   black pepper

For the classic puff pastry
250g/1¾ cups plus 2 Tbsp
   plain (all-purpose) flour,
   plus extra to dust
2 pinches of sea salt
250g/18 Tbsp butter, chilled
1 tsp lemon juice
125ml/½ cup water

Preheat the oven to 180°C/350°F/gas mark 4. Roll out the puff pastry to 5mm/¼in thick and cut out 8 circles, 9cm/3½in in diameter. Place on a baking sheet lined with baking parchment and brush with the beaten egg. Using a knife tip, score a pattern onto each. Bake for 15–20 minutes, until well risen and golden brown. Take out of the oven and leave on a wire rack to cool.

Meanwhile, make the filling. Cut the asparagus into 2-cm/¾-in chunks. Heat the butter in a sauté pan, add the shallot and sauté for a few minutes, then add the wine and asparagus and simmer for 5 minutes. Add the peas and cream, and season. Simmer for 3 minutes, then take off the heat. Cut the puff pastry rounds in half and place the salad inside with the filling.

CLASSIC PUFF PASTRY

Sift the flour and salt into a bowl. Rub in 50g/3½ Tbsp of the butter with your fingertips until the mixture resembles crumbs. Add the lemon juice and water and mix quickly into a dough. Knead very briefly on a floured surface, just until smooth. Wrap in cling film and chill for 30 minutes.

Roll out the chilled dough on a floured surface to a rectangle around 50 x 30cm/20 x 12in. Slice the remaining cold butter and arrange over half the dough, 2cm/¾in from the short edge on one side of the dough, creating a 25-cm/10-in square of butter. Fold the 2-cm/¾-in edge over the butter then fold over the other side of the dough and gently press to encase the butter. Roll out to a rectangle, making sure the butter stays inside the dough. Now, take a short side of the rectangle and fold it over towards the centre by one-third; take the other short side and fold it over the top, as if you were folding a business letter. Wrap in cling film and leave to rest in the fridge for 15 minutes. Roll out to a rectangle once more and repeat the folding and chilling. Do this six times in total.

"BURNING LOVE" WITH SWEDE AND CARROT MASH

Here is how to have a super meal with a variety of vegetables that will do you good! For me this is just great, tasty comfort food that will sustain you through cold nights and is inspired by a classic dish that I grew up with: a mash served with onions and bacon fried in lot of fat – a dish called "burning love"!

SERVES 4–6

2 leeks
300g/10½oz scorzonera
200g/7oz kale
50g/about ½ cup walnuts, chopped
3 Tbsp extra virgin olive oil
3 garlic cloves, fine chopped
1 tsp coriander seeds, ground

For the swede and carrot mash
1 swede (rutabaga), about 500g/1lb 2oz
300g/10½oz carrots
1 small onion
1½ red chillies
75g/5 Tbsp butter
400ml/generous 1½ cups water
Sea salt and freshly ground black pepper

For the mash, peel the swede (rutabaga) and carrots and cut them into big chunks. Chop the onion and chillies. Melt 50g/3½ Tbsp of the butter in a large pan, add the swede, carrots, onion and chillies and sauté for 2–3 minutes. Add the water, cover and let it simmer for about 10 minutes or until the vegetables are cooked. Do not drain.

Using a balloon whisk, mix in the remaining butter and season with salt and pepper. Whisk until everything is well mixed but still lumpy.

While the vegetables for the mash are cooking, slice the leeks and rinse well. Peel the scorzonera and cut it into 2-cm/¾-in chunks. Chop the kale. Add the walnuts to a large, dry frying pan and toast a little until starting to brown. Add the olive oil, garlic and coriander seeds and let them cook for a few minutes, then add the leeks, scorzonera and kale. Season with salt and pepper and let it cook for 10 minutes, then serve with the swede and carrot mash.

CREAMY BARLEY WITH COURGETTE AND MUSHROOM

Grains cooked this way are often compared to a risotto, but there is a difference in how much starch rice releases compared to barley, and so the finished texture is not the same.

In Scandinavia, this creamy dish is a lot like the different porridges we eat. Porridge has been everyday food for centuries, and when I was growing up we had it for dinner once a week; often Monday would be porridge day in many households. It has become fashionable again, and in Copenhagen we even have a porridge restaurant called GRØD where they serve a lot of savoury dishes for dinner.

SERVES 4

1 courgette (zucchini)
2 Tbsp extra virgin olive oil
200g/7oz brown mushrooms
1 shallot, finely chopped
3 garlic cloves, finely
  chopped
1 Tbsp thyme leaves,
  chopped
250g/1⅓ cups barley
700ml/scant 3 cups water
50g/3½ Tbsp butter
50g/1¾oz Parmesan, grated,
  plus extra to serve
Sea salt and freshly ground
  black pepper
Chopped curly parsley,
  to serve

Cut the courgette (zucchini) into 5-mm/¼-in dice. Heat the oil in a large, deep-sided frying pan, add the courgette dice and sauté until starting to brown. Clean the mushrooms and cut them into quarters. Add the mushrooms, shallot, garlic and thyme and sauté for 5 minutes, then add the barley and stir well. Let it cook for a few minutes then add the water with salt and pepper to taste. Let it simmer, covered, for 20–25 minutes over a low heat, stirring and checking now and then that the water has not all evaporated, adding a little more if necessary.

When the barley is cooked, add the butter and Parmesan, check the seasoning and stir well. Serve right away, topped with extra grated Parmesan and some chopped parsley, with a salad on the side.

SPELT TART WITH SPINACH, JERUSALEM ARTICHOKES AND FETA

This tart is perfect for everyday cooking and not that hard to make, and when it's in the oven there's even time to watch the news, or read a book. Any leftovers are great the next day and can be taken to work for lunch. It's also perfect for when you have guests, as it can be made the day before, then heated up to serve.

SERVES 4–6

For the pastry
100g/¾ cup plain
  (all-purpose) flour,
  plus extra for dusting
100g/1 scant cup wholegrain
  stoneground spelt flour
1 tsp sea salt
75g/5 Tbsp butter, chopped,
  plus extra for greasing
75g/⅓ cup skyr (quark) or
  fromage frais

For the filling
200g/7oz Jerusalem
  artichokes
2 Tbsp olive oil
2 garlic cloves, chopped
500g/1lb 2oz fresh or frozen
  spinach
5 eggs, beaten
100ml/scant ½ cup full-fat
  crème fraîche
200g/7oz feta cheese,
  crumbled
1 tsp freshly grated nutmeg
1 tsp each sea salt and freshly
  ground black pepper

Begin with the pastry. Mix both flours with the salt in a large bowl, then rub in the butter with your fingertips. Mix in the skyr (quark) or fromage frais. Knead the dough lightly with your hands just until the ingredients are combined. (Alternatively, pulse all the ingredients together in a food processor, adding a little water if the dough does not come together.)

Roll the dough out on a floured surface and butter a tart tin or dish, about 28cm/10in in diameter. Use the pastry to line the tart tin, then refrigerate for 1 hour.

Preheat the oven to 180°C/350°F/gas mark 4. Line the pastry case with baking parchment and pour in baking beans or uncooked rice. Bake in the hot oven for 15 minutes, then remove the baking beans and parchment and bake for a further 5 minutes.

Meanwhile, make the filling. Peel the Jerusalem artichokes and cut them into 1.5-cm/½-in chunks. Heat the oil in a large saucepan, add the Jerusalem artichokes and sauté for 3–4 minutes, then add the garlic and let it cook for about 5 minutes; take off the heat. If using fresh spinach, rinse in cold water, then place in a separate saucepan over a medium heat and allow it to wilt. When it is just wilted, drain really well in a sieve.

Put the beaten eggs, crème fraîche, feta, nutmeg and salt and pepper into a large bowl and mix well with a wooden spoon. Fold in the drained spinach and Jerusalem artichokes. Pour the mixture into the pastry case, return it to the oven and bake for 30–35 minutes, or until the filling has set but retains a slight wobble. Serve right way with a nice salad, such as Råkost (see page 160).

SPINACH DUMPLINGS IN TOMATO SAUCE

Not very Scandinavian, you may think, but hardy spinach is in abundance here, especially in winter. This is comfort food indeed and will make you feel good on cold evenings.

SERVES 4
700g/1lb 9oz spinach
500g/2¼ cups ricotta
4 Tbsp cornflour (cornstarch)
½ tsp freshly grated nutmeg
2–3 Tbsp extra virgin olive oil
Sea salt and freshly ground
  black pepper

For the tomato sauce
1 leek
1 courgette (zucchini)
1 Tbsp olive oil
2 garlic cloves, finely
  chopped
1 x 400g tin/2 cups chopped
  tomatoes
100ml/scant ½ cup water
5 sage leaves
100ml/scant ½ cup cream

Rinse the spinach several times in cold water and drain in a colander, then cook until wilted in a large saucepan and drain again, squeezing out as much liquid from the leaves as possible. Chop finely and mix with the ricotta, cornflour (cornstarch) and nutmeg, with salt and pepper to taste. Scoop out tablespoons of the mixture and shape into little dumplings. Heat the olive oil in a frying pan and cook the dumplings for 3–4 minutes on each side. Set aside and keep warm.

For the tomato sauce, cut the leek into 1-cm/⅜-in slices. Cut the courgette (zucchini) in half lengthways and then into 1-cm/⅜-in slices. Heat the olive oil in a saucepan and sauté the garlic for 1 minute, then add the courgette and leek slices and sauté for further 2 minutes. Add the tomatoes, water and sage, and let it simmer for 5 minutes, then add the cream and let it simmer for a further 5 minutes. Season to taste, add the spinach dumplings to the sauce and gently combine.

Serve with rice or boiled grains.

RYE CRUST TART WITH BROCCOLI AND LEEKS

I believe that fibre from grains is an important part of our diet and that we should eat wholegrain where possible. This rye crust tastes really good, with a lovely texture from the grainy flour. It stays crisper than crusts made with white flours when baked with a filling, so is ideal in a tart.

SERVES 4–6

For the crust
100g/¾ cup plain
  (all-purpose) flour,
  plus extra for dusting
100g/1 scant cup wholegrain
  stoneground rye flour
1 tsp sea salt
75g/5 Tbsp butter, chopped,
  plus extra for greasing
75g/⅓ cup skyr (quark) or
  fromage frais

For the filling
300g/10½oz broccoli
500g/1lb 2oz leeks
3 garlic cloves, chopped
1 Tbsp olive oil
6 eggs
200g/¾ cup cottage cheese
200g/1 cup cream cheese
¼ tsp ground cloves
Sea salt and freshly ground
  black pepper

Begin with the pastry. Mix both flours with the salt in a large bowl, then rub in the butter with your fingertips. Mix in the skyr (quark) or fromage frais. Knead the dough lightly with your hands just until the ingredients are combined. (Alternatively, pulse all the ingredients together in a food processor, adding a little water if the dough does not come together.)

Roll the dough out on a floured surface and butter a tart tin or dish, about 28cm/10in in diameter. Use the pastry to line the tart tin, then refrigerate for 1 hour.

Preheat the oven to 180°C/350°F/gas mark 4. Line the pastry case with baking parchment and pour in baking beans or uncooked rice. Bake in the hot oven for 15 minutes, then remove the baking beans and parchment and bake for a further 5 minutes. Remove from the oven and increase the oven temperature to 200°C/400°F/gas mark 6.

Meanwhile, make the filling. Thinly slice the broccoli into flat little trees. Slice the leeks and rinse well. Blanch the broccoli slices in boiling water for 1 minute, drain well and set aside. Sauté the leeks and garlic in the olive oil for 5 minutes, and pour out any excess water from the leeks. Season with salt and pepper.

Beat the eggs together in a large mixing bowl, then stir in the cottage cheese, cream cheese and cloves. Fold in the leeks and pour the mixture into the pastry case. Now arrange the broccoli slices over the top in a beautiful pattern, pushing them down lightly. Bake for 30–35 minutes, or until the filling has set but retains a slight wobble. Serve right away with a salad, such as the Tomatoes with Goat Cheese Dressing salad on page 172.

CAULIFLOWER GRATIN
WITH BAKED TOMATOES

I find this cauliflower gratin makes a perfect midweek dinner. It's real comfort food; tasty and old-school in the best possible sense. I tend to adapt a lot of recipes from my family archives, and this is one of my mother's that she made with ham, that I have left out in my version. But if you feel the need for some meat, I recommend serving the gratin with slices of good-quality ham.

SERVES 4

1 cauliflower, about 600g/
  1lb 5oz
300ml/1¼ cups water
40g/3 Tbsp butter
75g/½ cup plus 1 Tbsp plain
  (all-purpose) flour
100ml/scant ½ cup whole
  milk
4 eggs, separated
Freshly grated nutmeg,
  to taste
Sea salt and freshly ground
  black pepper

For the dish
1 Tbsp butter
3–4 Tbsp breadcrumbs

For the baked tomatoes
500g/1lb 2oz cherry
  tomatoes on the vine
50ml/¼ cup extra virgin
  olive oil
2 garlic cloves, roughly
  chopped
1 tsp each sea salt and freshly
  ground black pepper

Cut the cauliflower into chunks and cook in the water for about 5 minutes, then drain, reserving the water. Set both aside. Preheat the oven to 200°C/400°F/gas mark 6.

Melt the butter in a saucepan, add the flour and stir into a smooth roux. Add the reserved cauliflower cooking water a little at a time, stirring after each addition to remove any lumps. Add the milk and stir again, then add salt, pepper and nutmeg to taste and remove from the heat. Leave to cool a little for a few minutes. Separate the eggs and add the egg yolks to the sauce and stir again. Fold in the cauliflower.

Butter an ovenproof dish and sprinkle half the breadcrumbs inside the dish. Now whisk the egg whites until stiff, then fold into the cauliflower mixture and transfer to the dish. Sprinkle the remaining breadcrumbs over and dot butter evenly over the top. Bake for 40 minutes.

While the cauliflower is in the oven, mix the cherry tomatoes with the olive oil, garlic, salt and pepper and place in a small ovenproof dish. Bake for 10 minutes alongside the gratin, towards the end of its cooking time, and serve both right away.

BROWN CABBAGE AND FERMENTED CABBAGE

Cabbage is a kind of national treasure in Scandinavia, and has played an important role in our food culture and survival for centuries. Now that fermenting has created so much interest worldwide, cabbage is back. These are two of my cabbage recipes: a slowly cooked one and a fermented one. Both are time-honoured recipes, and when I start preparing them the smell reminds me of visits to homes of relatives when I was a little girl.

BROWN CABBAGE (BRUNKÅL)

SERVES 6–8

1.5kg/3½lb white cabbage
75g/5 Tbsp butter
50g/¼ cup caster (granulated) sugar
1 tsp black peppercorns
2 tsp allspice
2 tsp caraway seeds
2 bay leaves
10 thyme sprigs
Sea salt and freshly ground black pepper
  and lemon juice, to taste

Cut the cabbage into medium-thin slices. Melt the butter and cook until light brown, then add the sugar and let it melt into a light brown caramel. Stir well, then add the cabbage, spices and herbs and stir well. Reduce the heat to low, cover and let it simmer for about 2 hours. Take off the heat and season to taste with salt, pepper and lemon juice.

TIP

If you like things sweet and spicy, add some green chilli.

FERMENTED CABBAGE (SURKÅL)

MAKES 1 JAR

1 white cabbage, about 1kg/2lb 3oz,
  1 whole leaf reserved
20–30g/¾–1oz sea salt
2 apples
2 tsp caraway seeds
1 tsp allspice

Grate the cabbage and place it in a big mixing bowl with the salt. (Salt can be added according to your preference, so taste as you go along.) Using your hands, massage the cabbage, really giving it a good rub, for 5–10 minutes, until the juices come out into the bowl and the cabbage is soft. Grate the apple and add to the cabbage with the spices and transfer to a sterilized 1-litre/2-pint glass preserving jar. Place the reserved whole cabbage leaf on top, pushing down on it a little so it is covered by the liquid. Close the jar and store in a cool, dark place for 21 days, opening the jar every day for the first 5–7 days to let the gas out. Serve after 21 days, and store in the refrigerator.

WHOLE BAKED CELERIAC AND CAULIFLOWER

Tasty and easy to make, this dish also looks great, and people are always so surprised about how flavourful the vegetables taste. A lot of vegetables benefit from being cooked slowly and whole.

SERVES 4

For the celeriac
1 whole celeriac
50ml/¼ cup extra virgin
  olive oil
2–3 Tbsp coarse sea salt

For the cauliflower
1 whole cauliflower
50ml/¼ cup extra virgin
  olive oil
Sea salt and freshly ground
  black pepper

Preheat the oven to 160°C/325°F/gas mark 3.

For the celeriac, wash it and cut the base off if the roots are still muddy, leaving the skin on. Place on a baking sheet lined with baking parchment, pour over the olive oil and rub in the salt. Bake for 2 hours. Depending on size, sometimes a celeriac will need longer in the oven. Test if it is done by sticking a skewer into it – it should be soft in the middle.

For the cauliflower, rinse it and remove most of the outer leaves, with a few left on. Place on a baking sheet lined with baking parchment, pour over the olive oil and sprinkle with salt and pepper. Bake for 2 hours, basting it now and then with the olive oil.

WARM BUTTERNUT SQUASH WITH ALMONDS AND HERBS

Scandinavian food has taken me around the world as a cook. All the things I eat inspire me, and I like to bring home ideas and adjust recipes to my own traditions, seasons or availability – one of the best ways for cooking to evolve. I had a dish similar to this one in Seoul, Korea, and this is my Scandic autumn version for the time of year when pumpkins start to be harvested.

SERVES 4

1 butternut squash, about
   800g/1lb 12oz, unpeeled
2 Tbsp extra virgin olive oil
Sea salt and freshly ground
   black pepper
Watercress, to decorate

For the herb topping
2 spring onions (scallions)
1 green chilli, chopped
3 Tbsp chopped parsley
3 Tbsp chopped mint
1 garlic clove, grated
1–2 Tbsp lemon juice
2 Tbsp butter
100g/¾ cup almonds,
   roughly chopped

Preheat the oven to 180°C/350°F/gas mark 4.

Cut the butternut squash in half lengthways, scrape out all the seeds, then cut each squash half into slices from the shorter side. Place on a baking sheet lined with baking parchment, toss with the olive oil and some salt and pepper and bake in the oven for about 15 minutes.

Meanwhile, make the herb topping. Thinly slice the spring onions (scallions). Mix the chilli, chopped herbs, garlic and lemon juice together and set aside. Melt the butter in a frying pan, add the almonds and spring onions and cook until browned. Take off the heat and keep warm.

Transfer the cooked butternut squash slices to a serving dish, stir the herb mixture into the brown buttered almonds and spring onions, then spoon on top of the butternut squash. Finish by decorating with watercress.

KALE MASH WITH SPROUT AND APPLE STIR-FRY

I like Brussels sprouts – even when over-cooked, brown and a bit smelly. But I prefer them al dente so they keep that fresh, green, nutty flavour. Mash is a favourite in winter in cold places; it gives you comfort in a special way. I love any mash with a vegetable stir-fry, and you can kind of use any vegetables you have, so if you need to clean out your vegetable drawers in the fridge, this is the perfect dish.

SERVES 4

For the mash
600g/1lb 5oz potatoes
400g/14oz celeriac
2 garlic cloves
100g/3½oz kale
50g/3½ Tbsp butter
Sea salt and freshly ground
  black pepper

For the stir-fry
400g/14oz Brussels sprouts
2 leeks
2 apples
2–3 Tbsp extra virgin olive oil
3 garlic cloves, chopped
1 tsp freshly grated nutmeg

For the mash, peel the potatoes and celeriac and cut into large cubes. Chop the garlic. Put the potatoes, celeriac and garlic into a large saucepan, cover generously with water, bring to the boil and let them simmer for 25 minutes. Chop the kale, add to the pan and let it simmer for a further 5 minutes. Drain, reserving 100ml/scant ½ cup of the cooking liquid. Mash together with a balloon whisk and, while the mixture is still lumpy, add the butter with the reserved cooking water. Stir with a spoon and add salt and pepper to taste.

While the potatoes and celeriac are boiling, make the stir-fry. Cut the bases off the sprouts, then press each sprout down between your hands, and give it a light push so that the outer leaves loosen. Gently peel these off and set aside. Cut the inner part of each sprout in half or quarters. Slice the leeks and rinse well. Slice the apples.

Heat the oil in a big sauté pan, add the leeks, halved sprouts, garlic and nutmeg and sauté for 5 minutes, then add the apples and stir-fry for another 3 minutes. Add the sprout leaves, season to taste with salt and pepper and serve with the mash.

LONG SUMMER NIGHTS

I live in the centre of Copenhagen in a neighbourhood that in many ways feels like living in a small village in the heart of a big town. It consists of very narrow rows of small townhouses, and in the middle of each is an area with no cars, just a communal space with trees and tables for the residents. The children can play, neighbours can eat and hang out or have parties: it's a very cherished space. In front of each house we each have a small garden where life is lived, if weather permits, and it is here that I love to entertain. One of my favourite events is to eat langoustine, when in season, all evening. Friends and neighbours come over, we barbecue (grill) the langoustine, drink champagne, and eat it with bread and dips – very simple and so delicious.

BARBECUED LANGOUSTINES WITH LEMON MAYO AND CHILLI CREAM

Langoustines are a luxury here; for me, they are a summer treat. They are not cooked in any fancy way, just grilled or baked for about 8 minutes, but there have to be lots and they have to be served as simply as possible. That is the true Scandinavian seafood tradition. Langoustines are more or less available all year around, but the high season is July and August. They are plentiful on islands like Læsø and Anholt, which is a treasured summer destination in Denmark.

SERVES 6

60–70 fresh langoustines
1 whole head of garlic, cloves separated, peeled and chopped
2 lemons, sliced
4–5 Tbsp extra virgin olive oil
Sea salt and freshly ground black pepper

For the lemon mayo
300ml/1¼ cups Mayonnaise (see right)
3–4 Tbsp lemon juice
1 Tbsp finely grated unwaxed lemon zest

For the chilli cream
200ml/¾ cup Mayonnaise (see right)
100ml/½ cup full-fat crème fraîche
1 red chilli, chopped
1 garlic clove, finely grated

To serve
Lemon and lime wedges
1 loaf of Sourdough Bread, sliced (see page 224 for homemade)

For the lemon mayo, mix all the ingredients together in a small bowl, seasoning to taste with salt and pepper. Mix the chilli cream ingredients together, with salt and pepper to taste, in a separate small bowl. Set both aside in the fridge until ready to serve.

Place the langoustines in a large bowl and mix in the garlic and lemon slices. Drizzle with the oil, mix and sprinkle with salt and pepper.

Heat the barbecue (grill) and barbecue the langoustines for 8–12 minutes, depending on size, turning them regularly. Serve right away, with the lemon mayo, chilli cream, lemon and lime wedges, and bread.

MAYONNAISE
MAKES ABOUT 350ML/1½ CUPS

2 egg yolks
1 Tbsp Dijon mustard
1 tsp white wine vinegar
300ml/1¼ cups neutral-tasting oil, such as grapeseed
Sea salt and freshly ground black pepper

Whisk the egg yolks in a bowl, then add the mustard and vinegar and whisk together for 5 minutes. I prefer to use a food processor or hand mixer for this.

Gradually add about half the oil, very slowly at first, whisking continuously, until thickened and emulsified. Continue adding the remaining oil gradually, whisking continuously. Season with a pinch each of salt and pepper. Store in a sterilized jar in the fridge for up to 1 week.

RASPBERRY AND REDCURRANT TART

My summer parties are always about celebrating the season, so for my summer langoustine dinner, I always make a pudding with fresh red berries. They are available for such a short time, so I think the more you can eat the better. I make a very easy raw cream, which is light and tasty. If you do not eat raw yolks, it can be made without.

SERVES 6–8

For the pastry
200g/1½ cups plain
    (all-purpose) flour
50g/⅓ cup icing
    (confectioners') sugar
100g/7 Tbsp cold butter,
    chopped
½ egg, lightly beaten

For the chocolate coating
150g/5oz dark chocolate
    (60% cocoa)
10g/2 tsp butter

For the cream
2 egg yolks
2 Tbsp caster (superfine)
    sugar
200ml/¾ cup full-fat
    crème fraîche
1 vanilla pod (bean)
2 Tbsp finely grated unwaxed
    lemon zest
About 2–3 Tbsp lemon juice

For the berries
300g/10½oz raspberries
100g/3½oz redcurrants

Start by making the pastry. Sift the flour and icing (confectioners') sugar into a mixing bowl. Rub the butter in with your fingers until the mixture resembles crumbs. Add the egg and mix in to form a dough. Roll it out until large enough to line the base and sides of a tart tin 25cm/10in in diameter. Line the tin with the pastry. Wrap in cling film and chill for 30 minutes.

Preheat the oven to 180°C/350°F/gas mark 4.

Line the pastry case with a sheet of baking parchment and fill with baking beans or uncooked rice. Bake blind for 15 minutes, then remove the beans and baking parchment and bake for a further 15 minutes, then allow it to cool down.

Melt the chocolate and butter for the chocolate coating in a bowl over a pan of gently simmering water. When melted, mix until smooth, then spread over the baked tart case with a spatula, including up the sides. Leave to to set and cool.

For the cream, split vanilla pod (bean) in half lengthways and scrape out the seeds with the tip of a sharp knife. Place in a bowl with the remaining ingredients and beat together to a thick fluffy cream. Season to taste with more lemon juice.

Spoon the cream in the chocolate-coated tart case and spread out evenly, place all the raspberries on top and decorate with the redcurrants. Serve right away.

SOUPS FOR
EVERY SEASON

Soup is hygge food, and I do cook a lot of it in the colder months. It's a lovely way to serve bread, and I am a very big fan of bread. When I roast a chicken, I will use the carcass for a stock and freeze it for later use – for a noodle or mushroom soup, or a combined chicken and vegetable soup.

I often save all kinds of root vegetables and a few potatoes, and then cook them for a tasty leftover soup. When people come over to eat they ask for the recipe. I have to say "Sorry, no recipe, only my leftovers".

What I am trying to emphasize here is that all the odd vegetables that are left over from cooking during the week can be cooked together for a great soup. I am very keen on not wasting food, first of all because it's absurd we use so much energy to produce it and then waste it, and our planet can't sustain it. But also, for your own home economy, you can save money by cutting waste, and then spend that on organic meat, or something more expensive like artisan cheese.

Soup was for years a first course served to make sure people weren't too hungry when the main course arrived and meat was served; meat was very costly and therefore not served in big portions. I think some of the old ways of understanding how to put meals together would be great to reapply to today's way of living. Soup, bread and salad constitute an amazing meal, and I often like to cook two days' worth of soup, because I love the days when you come home from work and just have to heat up the dinner from yesterday.

FISH SOUP, MY CLASSIC WAY

This recipe recalls a time that no longer exists. In Scandinavia, famous artists would go to seaside hotels for fresh air and a change of scenery and society; the bourgeoisie and nouveau riche needed a break from city life. In those times when we lived more according to Proust, a fish soup like this would be served. Good fish soup always starts with a stock, which takes a little time to prepare, so a recipe like this is good for a dinner party, with the reward in the taste.

SERVES 6

½ tsp saffron strands
500g/1lb 2oz clams, preferably Venus clams
10 langoustines
400g/14oz white fish
2 Tbsp butter
3 garlic cloves, finely chopped
1 shallot, finely chopped
2 leeks, thinly sliced
1 carrot, finely diced
200g/7oz celeriac, diced
2 Tbsp plain (all-purpose) flour
200ml/¾ cup dry white wine
2 litres/8½ cups hot fish stock (see below)
200ml/¾ cup double (heavy) cream
Sea salt and freshly ground black pepper
50g/1¾oz dill, chopped

Fish stock

2kg/4lb 6oz fish bones
4 garlic cloves
2 onions
1 fennel bulb
1 leek, with green tops
1 carrot
A few parsley sprigs
2 Tbsp olive oil
3 bay leaves
10 whole black peppercorns
1 Tbsp sea salt

Place the saffron in a small bowl, pour over a little boiling water and leave to infuse.

Clean the clams by thoroughly scrubbing them under plenty of running water, and discarding any that are broken or don't close tightly when you tap them. Place the clams in a saucepan, cover and cook for 8 minutes, then set the pan aside, covered.

Shell the langoustines and set aside. Cut the white fish into smaller pieces.

In a big saucepan, melt the butter then sauté the garlic, shallot, leeks, carrot and celeriac for a few minutes. Add the flour and stir well, then add the white wine and stir well again. Add the stock and saffron, with its soaking liquid, and the cream. Bring to the boil, turn down the heat and let it simmer for 5 minutes.

Add the clams with a slotted spoon, the langoustine and white fish, and let it simmer for 3–4 minutes more. Season to taste with salt and pepper, and serve sprinkled with the dill, and with some bread, like the Flute on page 214.

FISH STOCK

Rinse the fish bones and place in a stockpot. Roughly chop the garlic, onions, fennel, leek and carrot and add to the bones with 3–4 litres/3–4 quarts cold water. Bring to the boil, reduce the heat and let it simmer, uncovered, for 2 hours, then strain, discarding the bones and vegetables. Use right away or freeze for later use.

JERUSALEM ARTICHOKE AND LEEK SOUP WITH ARTICHOKE CRISPS

Some years ago I cooked this soup and forgot to add the cream that I usually included. When I served it I did not really understand the colour, but then when I sat down to dinner and tasted it, I realized what had happened, but did not change it because I liked it much better.

SERVES 4

1.5kg/3lb 5oz Jerusalem artichokes
500g/1lb 2oz leeks
2 garlic cloves, chopped
4 Tbsp extra virgin olive oil, plus extra for drizzling
1.5 litres/6⅓ cups water
3 bay leaves
1 tsp freshly grated nutmeg
Sea salt and freshly ground black pepper
1 litre/4⅓ cups cooking oil

Set aside 300g/10½oz of the artichokes and peel and dice the rest. Chop the leeks, using as much of the dark green tops as possible, and rinse in cold water. Sauté the garlic and leeks in 2 Tbsp of the olive oil then add the artichokes with the water, bay leaves, nutmeg and salt and pepper to taste. Cover, bring to the boil, then turn down the heat and let it simmer for 30 minutes.

While it is simmering, peel the reserved artichokes and cut into thin slices. Heat the oil in a deep frying pan, dry the slices with some kitchen paper, then deep-fry the slices in batches until golden brown. Drain on kitchen paper, then sprinkle with salt and pepper.

Remove the bay leaves from the soup then blitz until smooth. Taste for seasoning, then serve topped with the fried Jerusalem artichoke chips. Drizzle with a bit of extra virgin olive oil.

POTATO SOUP WITH TOASTED RYE FLAKES

As I always have potatoes and celeriac in my vegetable box during the winter, this is kind of my last-resort soup. For anybody who craves them, crisp fried bacon lardons are a great match.

SERVES 4

1.5kg/3lb 5oz potatoes
500g/1lb 2oz celeriac
1 leek, with green tops
1 green chilli
4 garlic cloves
1 rosemary sprig
2 bay leaves
1.5 litres/6⅓ cups water
Sea salt and black pepper

To serve

100g/3½ oz rye flakes
4 Tbsp chopped chives

Peel the potatoes and celeriac, and roughly chop them. Slice the leek and rinse well. Put all the vegetables and herbs in a large pan, add the water, cover and bring to the boil, then turn down the heat and let it simmer for 30 minutes.

Remove the bay leaves and rosemary sprig and blitz until smooth with a hand blender. It's very important not to use a food processor because it can make the soup very gluey. Season with salt and pepper to taste.

Toast the rye flakes in a dry frying pan and sprinkle over the soup with the chives to serve.

MUSHROOM SOUP

Autumn begins with this soup. If you have the chance to pick wild mushrooms, then this soup tastes wonderful with them. My mother picks them wild, and her mushroom soup is to die for.

SERVES 4

500g/1lb 2oz brown
  mushrooms
2 Tbsp butter
1 small onion, finely chopped
2 garlic cloves, chopped
2 Tbsp plain (all-purpose) flour
2 litres/8½ cups water or
  vegetable stock
100ml/½ cup double
  (heavy) cream
1 tsp freshly grated nutmeg
Sea salt and black pepper

Rinse and trim the mushrooms and split them into stems and caps. Dice the stems, slice the caps and keep separate. Melt the butter in a saucepan and sauté the diced stems with the onion and garlic. Add the flour and mix well, then add the water or stock and bring to the boil. Reduce and simmer for 45 minutes, then strain, discarding the solids, and pour back into the pan. Add the sliced mushroom caps and the cream, bring to the boil and let it simmer for 5 minutes.

Add the nutmeg and season to taste with salt and pepper. Serve topped with toasted flaked (slivered) almonds and thyme, and bread alongside.

NORDIC TOMATO SOUP WITH RYE

Madam Mangor was a Danish cook who, in 1837, wrote the country's first classic bestseller cookbook, changing the way the well-off middle classes cooked. Her testimony is still important today, as not only does it give us an insight into what was eaten in the 1800s, but the recipes are still used, even if they have inevitably changed over the years. The book includes a recipe for tomato soup which is smooth and sieved, and which Madam Mangor recommends serving with meat- or fish balls. Here is my tomato soup, which is quite different.

SERVES 4–6

200g/7oz rye grains
1 onion, diced
3 garlic cloves, finely chopped
200g/7oz celeriac, peeled and diced
1 carrot, peeled and diced
1 celery stalk, thinly sliced
2 Tbsp olive oil
3 x 400g cans/3 cups chopped tomatoes
2 Tbsp tomato purée (paste)
200ml/1 cup white wine
2 bay leaves
2 litres/8½ cups vegetable stock
Sea salt and freshly ground black pepper

To serve
1 small bunch of parsley, chopped

Rinse the grains in cold water and drain, then place in a saucepan and add cold water to cover the grains. Cover, bring to the boil, then let it simmer for 20 minutes. Drain and set aside.

In a large saucepan, sauté the onion, garlic, celeriac, carrot and celery in the olive oil for a few minutes, then add the tomatoes, tomato purée (paste), wine, bay leaves and stock, and bring to the boil. Let it simmer, covered, for 10 minutes then add the drained rye grains and season to taste with salt and pepper. Serve right away, sprinkled with parsley.

SPICY PUMPKIN SOUP WITH CROUTONS

Every Wednesday a box of organic vegetables arrives on my doorstep from a local company called *Aarstiderne*, which means "season". I love my box scheme. I am always so excited about it that I forget I actually pay for it; it seems like a gift. From September for a few weeks there is always a pumpkin in my box, so I have to come up with pumpkin recipes every week. Autumn is also the season for soup, and this is one of the classics.

SERVES 4–6

1 or 2 pumpkins (about 1.5kg/3¼lb peeled and deseeded flesh)
3 garlic cloves, finely chopped
1 large onion, chopped
75g/2¾oz fresh ginger, finely grated
1 red chilli, finely chopped
1 tsp cumin seeds
1 tsp coriander seeds
4 Tbsp olive oil
1 litre/4¼ cups vegetable stock
400ml/1¾ cups coconut milk
Juice of ½–1 lime
Sea salt and freshly ground black pepper

To serve
2 Tbsp extra virgin olive oil
2 slices of bread, cut into cubes
Fresh coriander (cilantro) or parsley

Preheat the oven to 180°C/350°F/gas mark 4.

Cut the pumpkin into chunks and place in an ovenproof dish with the garlic, onion, ginger, chilli, cumin and coriander seeds and olive oil, and mix well. Bake in the oven for 1 hour.

Remove the dish from the oven and transfer the pumpkin mixture to a saucepan together with the vegetable stock. Bring to the boil then let it simmer for 15 minutes. Add the coconut milk and blend the soup until smooth, adding more water if the soup is too thick – it will vary depending on the water content in the pumpkin. Bring gently to the boil again and season to taste with lime juice, salt and pepper.

Just before serving, heat the extra virgin olive oil in a frying pan, add the bread cubes and fry for a few minutes until golden brown, take off the heat and sprinkle with a little salt. Serve the soup with the croutons and the coriander (cilantro) or parsley sprinkled over.

CHICKEN SOUP WITH HERBS AND ROOT VEGETABLES

Chicken soup is pure love, I think. In most cultures chicken soup is what is needed when you are feeling down or just tired, or when you have flu. My chicken soup is a mix of my Scandinavian heritage and a bit of southern Europe, plus the all-important fresh herbs that we use a lot in cooking.

SERVES 4

200g/1 cup dried white beans, such as cannellini
3 Tbsp extra virgin olive oil
3 garlic cloves, chopped
300g/10½oz parsnip, finely diced
300g/10½oz Savoy cabbage, chopped
6 Tbsp chervil leaves, chopped
6 Tbsp parsley leaves, chopped
Sea salt and freshly ground black pepper

For the stock
1 chicken
3 bay leaves
2 celery stalks
1 carrot
1 onion, unpeeled
1 green chilli
4 garlic cloves
100g/3½oz fresh ginger
20g/¾oz sea salt
1 Tbsp whole black peppercorns
3 litres/3 quarts water

The day before making the soup, soak the dried beans in cold water overnight. The next day, drain them and cook in boiling water for 40 minutes until tender, then drain and set aside.

While the beans are cooking, put the chicken and the remaining stock ingredients in a stockpot, bring to the boil then reduce to a simmer, uncovered, for 1 hour. Remove the chicken from the stock and strain the stock. Pour the stock back into the pot and let it simmer until reduced to 2 litres/8½ cups.

Heat the olive oil in a big saucepan and sauté the garlic, then add the parsnip, cabbage and beans and sauté for a few minutes. Add the stock and bring to the boil. Skin the chicken and shred the meat off the bones. Save half the meat for another use, then add the other half to the soup, seasoning to taste with salt and pepper. Add the chervil and parsley and let it simmer for 2 minutes before serving.

CAULIFLOWER SOUP

This is perfect for a starter, but also for dinner during the week, and is really nice served with home-baked bread – there's something lovely about dipping your bread in soup. Soup is really important comfort food, especially when you live in a cold climate. Any soup can be spiced up with croutons, herbs, spices, nuts or any delicious toppings. Grilled prawns (shrimp) are also delicious with cauliflower soup.

SERVES 4

2 large heads of cauliflower
2 large potatoes, peeled
1 onion
3 garlic cloves, chopped
1 Tbsp butter
2 Tbsp extra virgin olive oil
1 litre/4 cups water
3 bay leaves
200ml/¾ cup double
   (heavy) cream

To serve

1 tsp butter
2 Tbsp capers
100g/¾ cup almonds,
   chopped
Rye breadcrumbs (or other
   breadcrumbs)
1 bunch of watercress

Roughly chop the cauliflowers, potatoes and onion, then put in a large saucepan with the garlic, butter and half the oil. Gently heat until the vegetables start to sizzle, then pour in the water and add the bay leaves and some salt and pepper. Cover, bring to the boil, lower the heat and let it simmer for 10–15 minutes.

Remove the bay leaves, add the cream and blitz until smooth. Reheat in the pan, adding more water if necessary to get the right consistency.

At the same time, melt the butter in a frying pan and add the capers, almonds and breadcrumbs. Sprinkle the mixture over the soup and top with watercress to serve.

ASPARAGUS SOUP

Spring has arrived when in early April you can get the first asparagus from Spain. A little later the local Danish asparagus arrives and then I start eating it several times a week, because it is so good. I can't recommend enough eating your local vegetables in season until you almost get sick of them, then moving on to the next thing; that way there's always something to look forward to.

SERVES 4

1kg/2lb 3oz asparagus spears
1 Tbsp butter
2 Tbsp extra virgin olive oil
1 onion, chopped
2 garlic cloves, chopped
1.5 litres/6⅓ cups water
Sea salt and freshly ground
  black pepper

To serve
1 Tbsp butter
8 quail's eggs, boiled and
  halved
100g/3½oz salmon roe
1 bunch of watercress

Because asparagus is grown in sandy water, make sure to soak them in water for 10 minutes before using, then trim the asparagus by holding the stalk with one hand at the bottom and bending it a few centimetres away with your other hand to snap off the tougher part. Now cut off the tips of the asparagus and set aside, and chop the stalks.

Heat the butter and oil in a large saucepan until foaming. Add the onion, garlic and asparagus stalks and let them cook for 2–3 minutes until softened but still bright. Pour in the water, bring to the boil and let it simmer for 10 minutes, then blitz until smooth.

Melt the butter in a frying pan, add the asparagus tips and fry for 1–2 minutes. Serve the soup topped with the asparagus tips, halved quail's eggs, salmon roe and watercress.

THE SALADS
I EAT

Historically, green salad was never a big part of Scandinavian food culture because it only grew for a few months in summer. The diversity in vegetables has also been limited and very seasonal because it was not possible a few hundred years ago to transport vegetables over long distances. But even with a challenge like that, old cookbooks and archives show that lots of different vegetables were served throughout the year – most of them locally grown.

In 1996 I founded my company, Hahnemanns Køkken. The whole concept is based around salads – not the green ones, but the vegetable salads where you make use of all vegetables, herbs and spices to create exciting ways of eating. This is the way I have enjoyed vegetables all my life. As a child I was lucky to be exposed to cooking from the whole world because of my parents' friends and their lifestyles. I experienced how spices, rare vegetables, beans and seasonal produce came together to create whole new ways of eating that were not traditional or in any comparable to how my grandparents ate. It was an alternative, cheap and very global approach; it was also a rebellion against the Scandi nuclear family meal of meat, potatoes and gravy, every day.

So when I got the idea for my company in the late 1990s, I thought the best way to increase the amount of vegetables we should eat every day was to focus on salads. Over the years, this way of eating has evolved immensely due to a lot of wonderful cooks' sharing of ideas. I have been so lucky to work with many of them, and they have all inspired me. Here in this chapter are some of my classic salads as well as some of my new favourites. I also recommend letting your leftover vegetables guide you.

RADICCHIO AND BLUEBERRIES

In the summer the woods in Sweden are full of berries and I love going on long walks on breezy summer days to pick blueberries. They taste completely different to the ones you buy: they are sweet and have a bit more acidity, and are blue all the way through. When you come home with your blueberry treasure, you have to use them within a few days, and a great way to make use of them is in salads or pan-fried to serve with fish or chicken.

SERVES 4–6

100g/¾ cup hazelnuts
1 radicchio head, leaves
  separated
15g/½oz mint leaves
3 sprigs of tarragon,
  leaves only
1 bunch of basil, leaves only
200g/7oz blueberries

For the dressing
1 Tbsp elderflower cordial
1 Tbsp white wine vinegar
1 Tbsp walnut oil

Preheat the oven to 180°C/350°F/gas mark 4. Roast the hazelnuts on a baking sheet in the oven until the skins start to loosen, then leave to cool. Rub off the skins with your hands, then roughly chop them.

Rinse the radicchio and all the herbs in cold water and drain and dry well, using a salad spinner if you have one. In a big mixing bowl, mix the salad and herbs together, then add the blueberries and hazelnuts.

To make the dressing, whisk the elderflower, vinegar and walnut oil together, and mix in the salad just before serving.

BUCKWHEAT, COURGETTES, TOMATOES AND LOVAGE

Buckwheat (kasha) grows as far away as Siberia and was for centuries eaten in Scandinavia, boiled into a porridge. Then, as we became wealthier, buckwheat disappeared except for its use in blinis. Now it is back again, roasted in soups or salads; it tastes both earthy and nutty, so is a great match for many vegetables.

SERVES 4

10g/2 tsp butter
100g/⅔ cup buckwheat (kasha)
2 courgettes (zucchini)
5 spring onions (scallions)
2 Tbsp extra virgin olive oil
400g/14oz tomatoes
1 small bunch of flat-leaf parsley
2 Tbsp chopped lovage
Sea salt and freshly ground black pepper

For the dressing
1 small garlic clove, crushed
2 Tbsp white wine vinegar
2 Tbsp chopped lovage

Melt the butter in a frying pan and fry the buckwheat (kasha) until crunchy and golden brown. Tip onto a plate lined with kitchen paper and leave to cool.

Cut the courgettes (zucchini) into slices at an angle and brush both the slices and the whole spring onions (scallions) with the olive oil. Sprinkle with salt and pepper and grill on both sides in a grill pan for 3–4 minutes or until golden. Leave to cool, then cut the spring onions in 4-cm/1½-in lengths. Cut the tomatoes in half, and pull the parsley leaves from the stalks, discarding the stalks.

Put the courgettes and spring onions into a big mixing bowl with the remaining ingredients, including the toasted buckwheat, and mix everything together.

To make the dressing, mix the garlic, vinegar and lovage together. If it is not acidic enough, season with more vinegar. Mix in the salad and add salt and pepper to taste just before serving.

JERUSALEM ARTICHOKE, SPRING ONIONS AND BELUGA LENTILS

Jerusalem artichokes are a quintessential winter vegetable – sweet and nutty and perfect in a salad served with soup for dinner. Danes go through tons of Jerusalem artichokes every winter. I think they are perfect for any everyday winter dish, as in this salad. But no matter what day of the week it is or what you are cooking, remember to set the table and light a candle. All meals are special.

SERVES 4

500g/1lb 2oz Jerusalem artichokes
3 Tbsp extra virgin olive oil
100g/3½oz black beluga lentils
1 spring onion (scallion)
250g/9oz small plum tomatoes
2 Tbsp parsley leaves
2 Tbsp white wine vinegar
Sea salt and freshly ground black pepper

Preheat the oven to 180°C/350°F/gas mark 4.

Rinse the artichokes well in cold water and cut into long slices, with the skins on. Place in a roasting tin lined with baking parchment, toss with the olive oil and some salt and pepper and roast for 20 minutes. Set aside to cool.

While the artichokes are in the oven, cook the lentils in boiling water with a pinch of salt added until just tender, then drain and leave to cool.

Slice the spring onion (scallion) very thinly on the diagonal. Cut the tomatoes in quarters and roughly chop the parsley. When everything is ready, put all the ingredients into a big mixing bowl, and use your hands to mix the salad lightly. Season to taste with salt and pepper and a little more vinegar if it is not acidic enough, and serve right away.

KOHLRABI, POMEGRANATE, WALNUTS AND RYE GRAIN

Lots of foods get lost in translation. In Danish kohlrabi is actually called "glass cabbage" because of its transparency when peeled. "Kohlrabi" is swede (rutabaga), which in Danish means a person from Sweden, so when I wrote my first recipe with kohlrabi I got it very wrong.

SERVES 4–6

150g/5¼oz rye grains
2 kohlrabi, about 300g/
 10½oz total weight
50g/½ cup walnut halves
2 pomegranates
50g/1¾oz rocket (arugula)

For the dressing

3 Tbsp pomegranate molasses
1 Tbsp apple cider vinegar
1 tsp honey
1 Tbsp extra virgin olive oil
Sea salt and black pepper

Cook the rye grains in plenty of boiling water until tender but still firm (depending on whether the grain is pearled or not, this can take anything from 20 minutes to 1 hour). Drain and leave to cool.

Peel the kohlrabi and cut into thin slices. Toast the walnuts in a dry frying pan for a few minutes, then chop. Remove the pomegranate seeds and save the juice, pressing the empty halves over a bowl to catch the juice. Put all the salad ingredients in a large bowl. Mix the dressing ingredients together, including the reserved pomegranate juice, and stir in the salad.

BRUSSELS SPROUT SALAD

Sprouts are lovely raw, and even though separating these hard little heads into leaves is time consuming, the resulting texture really creates a lovely salad. For anyone who hates over-cooked sprouts, here is a way to overcome their aversion to the little vegetable.

SERVES 6

400g/14oz Brussels sprouts
2 pomegranates
2 spring onions (scallions),
 thinly sliced
A big bunch of flat-leaf
 parsley, leaves only
2–3 Tbsp extra virgin olive oil
Sea salt and black pepper

Using a small, sharp knife, remove the middle stem from each sprout, then slightly press them and roll them around between your palms to loosen the leaves. Gently pull them apart so that the leaves stay intact, then set aside in a bowl of ice-cold water.

Remove the pomegranate seeds and save the juice, pressing the empty halves over a bowl to catch the juice. Drain the sprout leaves and add to a big mixing bowl. Mix in the pomegranate seeds and juice, with the spring onions (scallions), parsley leaves and oil, with salt and pepper to taste.

RYE, RED ONION, BEETROOT AND BLACKCURRANTS

Rye, mostly known for its use in bread, beer and whisky, really is a grain with a lot of potential, and can be used in cooking as well. I use it in salads and soups, or simply boiled instead of rice to serve with a stew. It can be combined with most vegetables, and is a great match with beetroot (beet). This salad is really good with lamb, chicken or duck.

SERVES 4–6

150g/5¼oz rye grains
2 red onions
1 tsp sugar
Extra virgin olive oil
150g/5¼oz beetroot (beet)
100g/1 cup blackcurrants,
   defrosted if frozen
2 Tbsp balsamic vinegar
Sea salt and freshly ground
   black pepper
Fresh dill, to serve

Preheat the oven to 180°C/350°F/gas mark 4.

Cook the rye grains in plenty of boiling water until tender but still firm (depending on the grain this can take anything from 20 minutes to 1 hour), then drain.

While the rye grains are cooking, peel the red onions and cut them into wedges. Put them on a baking sheet lined with baking parchment, sprinkle with the sugar and some salt and pepper, and drizzle with a little olive oil. Roast for 10 minutes, then place in a big mixing bowl with the drained rye and leave to cool together.

Peel the beetroot (beet) and, using a mandolin, cut into super thin slices. Add to the rye and onions with the blackcurrants, balsamic vinegar and 1 Tbsp olive oil. Now mix well and season to taste with salt and pepper, and maybe also a little more balsamic, if it needs more acidity. Serve right away.

MY FAMILY'S BEAN SALAD

In the early 1980s, my mother started making a green bean salad with steamed beans mixed with red onions, bacon and vinaigrette. It was new, modern cooking and I loved it. I have always really liked beans of all sorts, including the white beans I often had as a child when the grown-ups cooked what, in the 1970s, was called hippie food. Later in the 1990s, when I started cooking professionally, I starting mixing white beans into salads. This was a new idea at the time, even though that seems hard to understand now. Cooking has evolved enormously over the last 30 years.

SERVES 4–6

150g/¾ cup dried white beans, such as cannellini
300g/10½oz fresh green beans
100g/3½oz radishes
50g/1¾oz flat-leaf parsley, leaves only

For the dressing

1 egg yolk
1 garlic clove, finely grated
4 Tbsp lemon juice
4 anchovies in oil
50ml/¼ cup grapeseed oil
100ml/½ cup Greek yogurt
Sea salt and freshly ground black pepper

The day before you make the salad, put the dried beans in a bowl, cover with water and allow to soak overnight.

The next day, drain the dried beans and cook in boiling water for about 45 minutes until tender, then drain and leave to cool. Cook the green beans in boiling, salted water for 3–5 minutes, then drain and tip into a bowl of cold water. Leave for 1 minute, then drain.

To make the dressing, blend the egg yolk, garlic, lemon juice and anchovies to a smooth paste, then add the oil a little at a time, blending after each addition. Season to taste with salt and pepper, then stir in the Greek yogurt.

Cut the green beans in half. Very thinly slice the radishes, with a mandolin if you have one. Mix the green beans and radishes with the white beans and parsley in a big mixing bowl, using your hands to mix the salad. Season to taste again with salt and pepper and perhaps a little more lemon juice, if needed for acidity. Serve right away, with bread and some baked tomatoes.

CAULIFLOWER, PRAWNS AND DILL

When I was growing up we ate cauliflower two ways: raw with a dip as a crudité, or in a gratin. Another very popular dish at the time was cauliflower in disguise – yes, that was its name: boiled cauliflower with white sauce, covered in prawns (shrimp). I must admit, I've never eaten it, as it did not really appeal to me, but it has inspired me to make this great-tasting summer prawn salad.

SERVES 4–6

1 small cauliflower, about
   400g/14oz trimmed weight
10 radishes
200g/7oz cooked peeled
   prawns (shrimp)

For the dressing
6 Tbsp chopped dill
6 Tbsp chopped chives
150ml/⅔ cup Greek yogurt
1 Tbsp grated unwaxed
   lemon zest and 1–2 Tbsp
   juice
Sea salt and freshly ground
   black pepper

Cut the cauliflower florets and stalk into thin slices, rinse well in cold water then drain in a colander. Slice the radishes.

Mix all the dressing ingredients together, with salt and pepper to taste.

Mix the cauliflower slices, radishes and prawns (shrimp) together in a big mixing bowl, then mix in the dressing. Season to taste with salt and pepper and perhaps a little more lemon juice for acidity. Leave for 10 minutes then season again and serve.

PAN-FRIED SUMMER CABBAGE, RADISHES, BACON AND PEA SHOOTS

Summer cabbage served in a white sauce seasoned with nutmeg used to be an all-time classic with my *mormor*, or maternal grandmother. She would serve it with new potatoes and *frikadeller*. The summer cabbage has a lovely sweet flavour that is brought out even more when fried in butter, making a dish in its own right. I also like to use it – fried or raw – in salads, and eat it several times a week when it's in season. Then I will always think of my *mormor* and our time together in our beach house.

SERVES 4–6

100g/3½oz bacon lardons
1 pointed cabbage
1 Tbsp butter
10 radishes
175g/1¼ cups freshly shelled
  peas
50g/1¾oz pea shoots

For the dressing
1 Tbsp white wine vinegar
1 Tbsp Dijon mustard
1 small garlic clove,
  finely grated
1 tsp finely grated shallot
1 tsp honey
3 Tbsp extra virgin olive oil
Sea salt and freshly ground
  black pepper

Fry the bacon lardons in a frying pan until golden brown, using a little oil if necessary, then tip onto a plate lined with kitchen paper to drain the fat off a little. Cut the cabbage in long strips, 2cm/¾in wide. Slice the radishes.

Now make the dressing. Whisk the vinegar, mustard, garlic, shallot and honey together, then add the oil gradually and season to taste with salt and pepper.

Melt the butter in a frying pan, add the cabbage and cook until browning at the edges. Transfer to a serving platter, and straight away sprinkle the lardons, radishes and peas evenly over. Drizzle the dressing over the warm salad, top with the pea shoots and a grinding of pepper and serve right away.

CHICORY, PEARS AND GRAPES

Chicory (endive) is called Christmas salad in Danish. We never really ate it growing up, so for me it stayed a Christmas speciality until I travelled to Italy and ate it cooked. It was a revelation. This is my modern take on my family's Waldorf salad recipe.

SERVES 4–6

2 chicory (endive)
2 pears
300g/10½oz green grapes
1 celery stalk
50g/½ cup walnut halves

For the dressing
1 Tbsp Dijon mustard
1 tsp honey
2 Tbsp apple cider vinegar
2 Tbsp walnut oil
Sea salt and black pepper

Slice the chicory (endive) and pears and place in a big bowl. Cut the grapes in half and remove the seeds if necessary. Thinly slice the celery. Toast the walnut halves in a dry frying pan for a few minutes, then chop and allow to cool.

Put all the salad ingredients into a mixing bowl.

To make the dressing, whisk the mustard, honey and vinegar together, then gradually add the oil to emulsify, and season with salt and pepper. Mix in the salad just before serving.

DANISH RAW SALAD (RÅKOST)

Raw vegetables are healthy and tasty, and some root vegetables are quite inexpensive, so they make great salads when lettuce is expensive and tastes of nothing. I used to have a salad like this in my lunchbox in the 1970s, and I was mortified, as my classmates had rye bread with salami. That was too traditional for my hippie parents, so I told my classmates that I had a rare stomach condition and had to eat this salad. Now I am thankful I grew up on such a diverse diet.

SERVES 4

400g/14oz celeriac
400g/14oz apples
1 Tbsp mustard seeds
2 tsp nigella seeds
1 Tbsp apple cider vinegar
1 Tbsp honey
Sea salt and black pepper

Peel and finely grate the celeriac and finely grate the apples with their skin on, leaving just the core out.

Toast the mustard seeds briefly in a dry frying pan. Mix everything together in big mixing bowl, with salt and pepper to taste. Serve right away, because it starts browning quite fast.

CLASSIC POTATO SALAD

Potato salad in summer, made with new potatoes, is a favourite among most people in Scandinavia. I like new potatoes and eat them often during the season. If they are newly dug, I don't need anything with them other than some salted butter and dill – a sublime meal, but here I have used them in a more elaborate way. There is traditional Danish recipe for warm potato salad just with cooked onions and vinegar, which is quite sweet, and this is my modern version of it.

SERVES 4

600g/1lb 5oz new potatoes, such as Jersey royals, unpeeled
2 sweetcorn cobs
1 small red onion
3 Tbsp white wine vinegar
50g/1¾oz mustard leaves
1 small bunch of basil, leaves only

For the dressing
4 Tbsp white wine vinegar
2 Tbsp Mayonnaise (see page 120 for homemade)
4 Tbsp chopped dill
2 Tbsp crème fraîche
2 Tbsp capers, chopped
Sea salt and freshly ground black pepper

Mix all the ingredients for the dressing together, with salt and pepper to taste, and set aside.

Wash the potatoes and slice them. Cook in boiling, salted water for 5–8 minutes or until tender but still holding their shape.

While the potatoes are boiling, slice the kernels off the sweetcorn cobs by cutting vertically down each side of the cobs so all the kernels fall off. Thinly slice the onion into rings. Put the corn kernels in a pan with the onion slices and vinegar and boil for 2–3 minutes.

Drain the potatoes. While they're still warm, mix with the red onion and corn kernels, then mix in the dressing. Finally, mix in the mustard and basil leaves. Serve right away while still warm.

LEFTOVER BEEF SALAD

This beef salad was one of the first recipes I wrote after I got my first column as a food writer in a Danish magazine. It's more than 10 years ago now, but I have never tired of this recipe – some recipes you forget and some stick with you. If you don't have leftover beef, buy steak and fry it medium-rare. It's a great salad for parties where you serve it buffet style.

SERVES 4

500g/1lb 2oz leftover roast beef
150g/5¼oz parsley root or parsnip, peeled
1 Tbsp olive oil
2 small Romaine lettuces, leaves separated
50g/1¾oz mustard leaves
Sea salt and freshly ground black pepper

For the dressing

1 tsp Dijon mustard
½ tsp honey
1 Tbsp chopped mint
2 Tbsp chopped tarragon
1 Tbsp tarragon white wine vinegar
1 Tbsp grapeseed oil or other neutral-tasting oil

Preheat the oven to 180°C/350°F/gas mark 4.

Start by making the dressing. Whisk together the mustard, honey, herbs and vinegar, then whisk in the oil gradually and season to taste with salt and pepper.

Cut the beef into strips, mix with the dressing and leave for 30 minutes, to enhance the flavours.

Meanwhile, cut the parsley root in half and then into sticks about 1cm/⅜in thick and 5cm/2in long. Mix with the olive oil and some salt and pepper and spread out in a roasting tin. Roast in the oven for 15 minutes then leave to cool.

Just before serving, mix the beef with the lettuce and mustard leaves and the parsley root then place on a serving dish and serve right away.

BRUSSELS SPROUTS, CHILLI AND ORANGES

The old apprehension about Brussels sprouts is disappearing, maybe not fast but steadily, after more and more people discover that you do not have to eat them after they have been cooked to death and turned brown. They are delicious al dente and even raw, and as with most members of the cabbage family, they can be paired with endless combinations of flavours. Here is a real winter recipe with lots of flavours to warm you up. It tastes really good with fish such as steamed cod, or grilled prawns (shrimp).

SERVES 4

300g/10½oz Brussels
  sprouts
2 Tbsp extra virgin olive oil
1 red chilli, sliced
Juice of ½ lime
50g/1¾oz pine nuts
4 oranges
50g/1¾oz coriander
  (cilantro)
Sea salt and freshly ground
  black pepper

Cut the sprouts into quarters, rinse in cold water and drain well. Heat the oil in a frying pan and sauté the sprouts with the chilli for 5 minutes, adding a few spoonfuls of water if they start to stick to the pan and burn. Transfer to a mixing bowl and reserve the pan. Pour the lime juice over the sprouts and leave to cool.

Toast the pine nuts in the same pan over a medium heat for a few minutes or until golden, then leave to cool and add to the mixing bowl.

Cut the peel off the oranges and then cut them into slices. Add the oranges and coriander (cilantro) to the bowl and mix (using your hands to toss the salad is best). Season to taste with salt and pepper, adding more lime juice if necessary, for acidity. Serve right away.

NORDIC QUINOA SALAD

I will admit I have not grown to be quinoa's biggest fan, and so don't cook with it a lot. It has, however, found its way into this salad because I ran out of spelt grains, and in the back of my grains cupboard I found a bag of red quinoa that I had never used. To my delight it was not too old, so I gave it a go and it turned out to be delicious. Now I use it for lunch, just a stand-alone salad, or for a lot of other different things like roast pork and frikadeller.

SERVES 6

100g/½ cup red quinoa
100g/3½oz kale
100g/3½oz red cabbage
1 celery stalk
3 dessert apples, such as Cox
50g/½ cup walnut halves

For the dressing
1 Tbsp Dijon mustard
1 Tbsp honey
4 Tbsp apple cider vinegar
2 Tbsp walnut oil
Sea salt and freshly ground
  black pepper

Cook the quinoa in plenty of boiling water for 15 minutes or until cooked, then drain well and leave to cool before transferring to a big salad bowl.

Cut the kale into medium-thin slices, thinly slice the cabbage and celery, and slice the apples. Toast the walnut halves in a dry frying pan for a few minutes, then chop. Allow to cool.

Mix all the salad ingredients into the salad bowl (the best way to do this is with your hands).

To make the dressing, whisk together the mustard, honey and vinegar, then whisk in the oil gradually and season to taste with salt and pepper. Mix the salad with the dressing just before serving.

KOHLRABI AND CUCUMBER

Kohlrabi has a fresh, sweet kind of light taste. Eating it raw like carrots or using it in salads is very much inspired by the Asian kitchen. I also like to use ginger raw in salads. When I cook everyday meals I focus firstly on whether my main ingredients are in season, and then after that I want to bring the world into my kitchen, and I really enjoy the diversity of flavours. It is interesting: when you look at old Scandinavian cookbooks, they used spices in both cooking and baking, and ginger was often used in preserving. The spices travelled up through Europe from the New World then ended up in Hamburg, a trading centre for Scandinavia and a bridge to a bigger culinary world.

SERVES 4

400g/14oz kohlrabi
2 cucumbers
50g/1¾oz cashew nuts
A small bunch of chives
Freshly ground black pepper

For the dressing
2 Tbsp freshly grated ginger
2 Tbsp soy sauce, plus extra
   to serve
1 tsp honey
1 Tbsp sesame oil
2 Tbsp lime juice, plus extra
   to serve

Peel and halve the kohlrabi, then cut it into thin slices and place it in a big mixing bowl. Cut the cucumbers lengthways, scrape out the seeds, cut into slices 5mm/¼in thick and add to the kohlrabi. Toast the cashew nuts in a dry frying pan for a few minutes, then roughly chop and allow to cool. Cut the chives into 5-cm/2-in lengths. Add to the bowl.

Now make the dressing. Whisk all the ingredients together and mix in the salad just before serving. Add pepper and soy sauce to taste, and perhaps a little lime juice for acidity and serve right away.

TOMATOES WITH GOAT CHEESE DRESSING

You can grow tomatoes in Denmark in the summer, and I do that with my mother in a greenhouse at her house in the country, and in my own small greenhouse in Copenhagen. We grow about 10 to 15 different kinds, and we experiment a lot with different varieties to find out which ones we think taste the best here in our climate. We have been quite successful with cherry tomatoes, both red and yellow, and this recipe is a great summer salad using our greenhouse tomatoes. The best way to enjoy this salad is outside for lunch, with rye bread and butter.

SERVES 4

500g/1lb 2oz cherry
   tomatoes, red and yellow
2 sprigs of fresh tarragon,
   leaves only
Edible flowers, to decorate
   (optional)

For the dressing
30g/1oz soft goat cheese
75g/2½oz Greek yogurt
2 Tbsp single (light) cream
Sea salt and freshly ground
   black pepper

For the croutons
3 thin slices of stale bread
1 Tbsp extra virgin olive oil

Mix all the ingredients together for the dressing, seasoning to taste with salt and pepper.

For the croutons, fry the bread in the olive oil on both sides until golden brown. Leave to cool and then break into smaller pieces.

Cut the tomatoes in half and place on a serving platter. Sprinkle over the tarragon leaves and croutons, add small dollops of the dressing and decorate with fresh edible flowers, if you have some. Serve right away.

COOKING IN MY KITCHEN

I never dreamt of being a cook. More than anything I wanted to be a mother, and as a profession I sought to be a writer. I enjoyed cooking, and have done so all my life, like I love to eat. But cooking kind of chose me. I've been good at it since childhood. I can taste; I can smell. From early childhood, I knew seasons and produce. I never questioned why we only have strawberries in July; I knew because I saw where they grew, and picked them. I tasted the lovely little juicy things right off the plant. That was a sensation every summer. In my memory, it seems like I was excited by every meal.

I have always existed in the creative zone between words and craftsmanship. If I look back, I can see that in the kitchen I was sure of myself. I moved around with confidence, even as a young person when nothing around me made much sense. Love and relationships were awkward, my parents were not present, studying was hard, just surviving seemed hard work, and there was no manual to it all. The kitchen was where all that anxiety disappeared and I became a person who knew what I wanted, and what the food should taste like in the end. I understood that cooking was a small journey each time, and I could figure out most of the time where it would lead me. Mistakes did not put me off; they encouraged me. I was never, ever interested in anything else than the daily meals.

I did not realize cooking could be a way to make a living, and I probably never will even though I have lived by it for more than 20 years. I am always on my way to the real things I was going to do eventually. While I still debate this, I enter my kitchen, I boil water, I grind coffee beans and fill my coffee pot, I light the candles on my dining table, turn on the radio, open the cupboard next to the stove and take my apron out; I hate cooking without an apron, I feel naked. Every time I go through that ritual, I feel things will be all right.

I designed my kitchen, and I wanted an open space, a place where everything was fitted around who I am, instead of me being forced to fit into my kitchen. I am a chaotic person in a structured way – I do not close cupboard doors, I keep stacks of china and a range of teacups; my pots and pans only fit if put back in place in a certain way.

I hoard: I am afraid not to have everything all the time. I call it "supply angst". So I need space and a long, wide kitchen table where stuff can pile up, but where there will still be space for me to work while surrounded by the things I have collected.

I always start my day in my kitchen. Before I get dressed, I walk downstairs and make tea. I have a teacup for morning tea, a coffee cup for any mood I may be in, a teacup for the evening, and cups for guests. I have six white, bone china cups;

my husband drinks everything out of them. I enjoy drinking from the right cup; it is never just a cup. The only real ritual or routine I have is that I get up in the morning and make English breakfast tea. I drink out of a big teacup with roses. When I travel, that is the only thing I really miss: my morning tea in my kitchen.

Eating is such a deep-rooted pleasure as soon as we human beings have passed beyond the necessity of surviving! Cooking is the link to that, because without it the pleasure is limited. That is one of the reasons why I believe in real cooking and in having no restrictions on the way I eat. I do not much care for any kind of diet other than common sense. In my kitchen, gluten and sugar are celebrated, and I talk to my sourdough. I eat everything and try not to eat too much, which is a daily challenge. The only rule in my kitchen is that the cooking has to be done with love. So, no matter if it's feeding myself a simple salad, or cooking a meal for my husband, or hosting a party, I keep that rule.

The gesture of love is always present. Imagine cooking for people you loathe – you would lose your appetite. The joy of eating is deeply rooted in our story, and often in our relationship with our mothers. I cooked for my children with a lot of love and sometimes with too much emphasis, not being able to compromise with their lunchbox and feeling miserable when they asked for ready-made things.

Compromising would have made my life easier. I could always handle criticism in my kitchen, but not from my children. I was instantly hurt if they did not think my food shook their world. I know they carry that with them. They know food sustains them and will probably always play an important role in their wellbeing.

I like to think civilization starts at the dinner table. Not to sound totally mad... but I do think all the conversations and exchanges of ideas coming out of my kitchen are important to keep striving to improve the world; and this applies not only to dinner at our house of course, but to all the dinners around the world. Dinner in my kitchen feels like time is carved out, and then all of sudden it runs out, people get up and leave, and you are left alone with your own reflections on the stories told, ideas presented.

Cooking is profoundly about living, so living in an era where the industry has taken over that part of people's lives is such an unimagined paradox. I think cooking is more important than ever for the connection with nature and life, but also for the repetition; that is, the space in your daily life it creates to do something meaningful – and again: not all meals can be ambitious, there have to be lots of simple meals cooked in a flash. The kitchen encompasses all of that: a space where the daily humdrum business of every day unfolds.

PICKLES, JAMS & CORDIALS

In my cupboards and fridge I store all the things I produce. I produce a lot more than I can eat, so I take them as gifts when I visit friends, which spreads a lot of joy! For a range of the recipes in this book, and Scandinavian cooking in general, preserves, pickled vegetables, jams and jellies are essentials. This is not only because of all the lovely things you can eat and combine them with, it is also because they are a way of prolonging any season. Previous generations did this out of necessity, to have food all through the year. We do not have to do that in our part of the world any more; we can just go and buy it in the stores. But it's not the same, and not just because they don't taste the same: there is a huge sense of satisfaction to be had in pickling and curing preserves.

I know it can be difficult to make time for this in our busy lives, so I always suggest to people that they gather a group of friends, organize the shopping, get the jars and all the equipment ready, and make a day of it. I promise, people will walk home happy and proud. They will treasure the produce, eat it with care and never throw it away, because they put love and time into it. Then they will always talk about how hyggelig the day was!

MY FAVOURITE PICKLES

ASIER (CLASSIC DANISH PICKLE)

2kg/4lb 6oz asier marrows
50–75g/3–5 Tbsp fine sea salt
1 dill flower, cut in 4

For the brine

1.5 litres/6 cups household vinegar or apple
    cider vinegar (5%)
750g/4 cups caster (granulated) sugar
2 Tbsp yellow mustard seeds
1 Tbsp black peppercorns
150g/5¼ oz very small shallots, peeled

Peel the asiers, cut them in half
lengthways, scrape out the seeds and cut
into 1-cm/½-in slices. Sprinkle with the
salt, cover with a clean tea towel and set
aside in a cool place for 2–3 hours.

Rinse the salted asier slices in cold water
and wipe them lightly with kitchen paper.
Place in 4 sterilized 500-ml/2-cup jars and
top with a dill flower. For the brine, bring
all the ingredients to the boil in a pan,
whisking until the sugar has dissolved. Pour
over the asier jars and immediately seal.
Leave for 3 weeks before eating.

PICKLED BEETROOT

1 kg/2lb 3oz small beetroot (beet)
Sea salt

For the brine

750ml/3¼ cups apple cider vinegar
400g/2¼ cups caster (granulated) sugar
1 Tbsp black peppercorns
1 Tbsp coriander seeds
2 bay leaves

Peel the beetroot (beet) and boil in salted
water for 15 minutes, checking after 10
minutes: they need to have some bite.

For the brine, bring all the ingredients to
the boil in a pan, whisking until the sugar
has dissolved. Take off the heat and cool.
Drain the cooked beetroot and, when cool
enough to handle, cut into wedges. Pack
in a sterilized jar, pressing them together,
pour the brine in, and seal immediately.
Leave for 3 weeks before eating.

PICKLED CUCUMBER

4 cucumbers
1 large dill sprig, in florets

For the brine

1 litre/4 cups spirit vinegar
400g/2¼ cups caster (granulated) sugar
2½ tsp sea salt
1 Tbsp mustard seeds
1 Tbsp black peppercorns

For the brine, bring all the ingredients to
the boil in a pan, whisking until the sugar
has dissolved. Take off the heat and cool.

Chop the cucumbers into 2-cm/¾-in slices
then pack with the dill into a sterilized
1-litre/4-cup jar, pressing them together.
Pour the brine in and seal immediately.
They are ready to eat the next day. Keep in
the fridge for up to 2 months once open.

PICKLED MIXED VEGETABLES

Pickled vegetables are great to have in the house. I use them for cold meat dishes and all kinds of open sandwiches. You can also drain off a few tablespoonfuls, chop them and mix with mayonnaise and some turmeric, for a homemade remoulade.

2kg/4lb 6oz rinsed and
  trimmed vegetables,
  such as broccoli, carrots,
  cauliflower, fennel, green
  beans, red onions, red (bell)
  peppers, spring onions
  (scallions)
100g/3½oz flaked sea salt

For the brine
1 litre/4¼ cups spirit vinegar
  (5%)
1 kg/5 cups light cane sugar
3 bay leaves
20g/¾oz black peppercorns
100g/3½ oz fresh
  horseradish, grated
100ml/scant ½ cup apple
  cider vinegar

Cut the vegetables into smaller pieces. Place them in a bowl and mix with the salt. Leave at room temperature for 3–6 hours.

Put the vinegar, sugar, bay leaves and peppercorns in a saucepan and let it boil until the sugar has dissolved. Press the salted vegetables into a 2-litre/2-quart, warmed sterilized jar, pour over the vinegar brine and leave to cool. Seal and keep in the refrigerator for up 3 months.

BERRY JAMS

Berries are a Nordic treasure: the range is amazing, and delicious berries are the joy of summer. They grow slowly in the cool climate and owe their especially good flavour to having so much daylight but not the strong sun that would make them grow too big. So less really is more...

GOOSEBERRY COMPOTE

1 vanilla pod (bean)
500g/1lb 2oz unripe gooseberries,
  topped and tailed
250g/1⅓ cups caster (granulated) sugar

Split the vanilla pod (bean) in half lengthways, then put it in a pan with the gooseberries and sugar. Bring to the boil, then reduce the heat and simmer for 20 minutes.

Pour the hot compote into warmed, sterilized preserving jars and, when cooled down, seal tightly and store in the refrigerator for up to 3 months.

RED GOOSEBERRY "JAM"

1kg/2lb 3oz red gooseberries,
  topped and tailed
500g/2 cups light cane sugar
1–2 vanilla pods (beans)
Finely grated zest of 2 unwaxed lemons

Preheat the oven to 150°C/300°F/ gas mark 2.

Place the gooseberries in an ovenproof dish and sprinkle with the sugar. Split the vanilla pods (beans) in half lengthways, then add them to the dish with the lemon zest and transfer to the oven.

Bake the gooseberries for 45–60 minutes, stirring every 15 minutes, until they have turned a rose-pink colour.

Pour the hot "jam" into warmed, sterilized jars and seal tightly. They will keep for months stored in a cold place.

STRAWBERRY-RHUBARB JAM

300g/10½oz strawberries
300g/10½oz rhubarb, thickly sliced
200g/generous 1 cup caster (granulated) sugar

Put the strawberries and rhubarb into a saucepan and bring to the boil gently. Boil, in the juice they release, for 10 minutes, then add the sugar and let it simmer for 10 minutes.

Pour into warmed, sterilized jars and seal tightly. This will keep for months stored in a cold place.

QUINCE, TWO WAYS

The quince is originally from the Caucasus, where it still grows wild today, and made its journey westwards across to the Mediterranean regions of Europe. It has the most beautiful little flowers when it blossoms in the spring, and the fruit is in season in October.

It is particularly popular in jams and jellies due to its high levels of pectin, and has become very popular again over the last decade. In Danish it is called *kvæde* and often gets dried and mixed in tea. Here I combine it with plum and serve it on my yogurt or porridge in the mornings, but also with cheese in the evening, or with roast duck.

QUINCE-PLUM "JAM"

10 green cardamom pods
2 cinnamon sticks
1 tsp coriander seeds
1.5kg/3lb 5oz quinces, peeled and cored
2 litres/8½ cups water
750g/3¾ cups light cane sugar
Finely grated zest and juice of 3 lemons
750g/1lb 12oz plums, stoned

Place all the spices in a square of muslin and tie to secure with string. Place the quinces, water, sugar, lemon zest and juice in a large saucepan with the spice bag, and bring to the boil. Cover and let it simmer until the quinces are al dente (test with a small, sharp knife). Using a slotted spoon, remove the quinces and plums from the liquid and leave to cool.

Reduce the liquid in the pan to 750ml/ 3¼ cups. Remove and discard the spices.

Chop the cooled quinces and plums into smaller pieces. Add the quinces to the boiling reduced syrup and boil for 1 minute, then add the plums and bring back to the boil for 1 minute.

Pour the hot jam into warmed, sterilized jars and seal. It will keep for months stored in a cold place.

QUINCE PURÉE

1kg/2lb 3oz quinces, peeled and cored
2 litres/8½ cups water
500g/2½ cups light cane sugar per
  1kg/2lb 3oz purée
Grated zest and juice of 2 unwaxed lemons

Place the quinces in a saucepan and add the water. Bring to the boil then cover and let them simmer until very tender when pierced with a small, sharp knife.

Remove the quinces from the water, weigh them and calculate the sugar quantity (see above). Transfer the quinces to a food processor and blend to a purée. Place the purée in a heavy-based saucepan and add the sugar, lemon zest and juice. Let them boil over a low heat, stirring constantly or it can easily burn, until the mixture thickens into a jam.

Pour the purée into warmed, sterilized jars and seal.

CONDIMENTS

These can be served with dishes, such as fried fish, game, meat, chicken or vegetable gratins, or added to gravies. In Sweden *lingon sylt* is eaten much as ketchup or mustard is in other cultures.

REDCURRANT JELLY

1kg/2lb 3oz redcurrants on their stalks
200ml/¾ cup water
850g/4¾ cups caster (granulated) sugar
  per 1 litre/4¼ cups liquid

Rinse the fruit in cold water and remove the stalks. Put the berries in a pan, add the water and bring to the boil. Reduce the heat, cover and simmer for 30 minutes. Don't stir! Pour the fruit and liquid into a jelly bag or sieve lined with fine muslin over a large bowl and strain overnight.

The next day, measure the juice and calculate the sugar needed. Add the sugar to the juice in a pan and let it simmer, uncovered, until drops of the liquid stick to the back of a spoon. Pour into warmed, sterilized jars and seal the following day. Store in a cool, dark place for 6 months.

ROSE JELLY

1 litre/4¼ cups tightly packed rose petals
1 litre/4¼ cups water
40g/1½oz powdered pectin or 150ml/
  10 Tbsp liquid pectin
1kg/5½ cups caster (granulated) sugar
Juice of 2 lemons

Gently rinse and drain the rose petals. Bring the water to the boil, add the petals, cover and boil for 15 minutes. Put the petals in a jelly bag or muslin-lined sieve over a large bowl and strain overnight. Do not press the bag or the jelly will be cloudy.

The next day, measure the liquid (discard the petals) and make it up to 1 litre/4¼ cups with cold water. Pour the liquid into a clean pan. Mix the powdered pectin with 2 Tbsp of the sugar and whisk it into the cold liquid (if using liquid pectin, just add it to the liquid). Bring to the boil over a medium-high heat, stirring. Add the lemon juice and remaining sugar and bring to the boil again, stirring. Boil over a medium-high heat for 8–10 minutes.

Pour into warmed, sterilized jars and seal.

LINGON SYLT

1kg/2lb 3oz fresh or frozen lingonberries
  or cowberries
200ml/¾ cup water
500g/2¾ cups caster (granulated) sugar

Boil the berries in the water for about 8 minutes, skimming off any scum. Add the sugar and boil for 8 minutes.

Pour into warmed, sterilized preserving jars.

RHUBARB, FOUR WAYS

In season I produce a lot of different things using rhubarb, and as well as eating them myself, I also give a lot away as a gift when invited to dinner, instead of a bottle of wine or flowers.

SWEET RHUBARB

500g/1lb 2oz rhubarb, rinsed
500ml/2 cups water
400g/2¼ cups caster (granulated) sugar
50g/1¾oz fresh ginger, thinly sliced
1 vanilla pod (bean), split in half lengthways

Trim and cut the rhubarb into 5-cm/2-in chunks. Place all the ingredients except the rhubarb in a saucepan. Bring to the boil and let it boil for a couple of minutes.

Put the rhubarb in a warmed, sterilized jar and pour the hot mixture over. Leave to cool, then seal and keep in the refrigerator for 3 weeks before using.

SOUR RHUBARB

500g/1lb 2oz rhubarb, rinsed
300ml/1¼ cups apple cider vinegar
10g/⅓oz black peppercorns
400g/1¼ cups caster (granulated) sugar
5 bay leaves
Grated zest and juice (about 150ml/⅔ cup) of 2 unwaxed lemons

Trim and cut the rhubarb into 5-cm/2-in chunks. Place all the ingredients except the rhubarb in a saucepan. Bring to the boil and let it boil for a couple of minutes.

Put the rhubarb in a warmed, sterilized jar and pour the hot mixture over. Leave to cool, then seal and keep in the refrigerator for 3 weeks before using.

RHUBARB COMPOTE

1kg/2lb 3oz rhubarb, rinsed
500g/2½ cups cane sugar
Grated zest and juice of 1 unwaxed lemon
2 vanilla pods (beans)

Trim and cut the rhubarb into 1-cm/
½-in chunks. Place the sugar, lemon zest and juice in a pan and heat until the sugar begins to melt, but without turning brown. Add the rhubarb and vanilla pods (beans) and let it simmer, stirring now and then, until the rhubarb pieces are lightly mashed and the sugar has completely dissolved.

Pour the mixture into a warmed sterilized jar and leave to cool.

RHUBARB CORDIAL

2kg/4lb 5oz rhubarb, rinsed
800ml/3¼ cups water
700g/scant 4 cups caster (granulated) sugar

Trim and cut the rhubarb into small pieces. Put it in a pan, add the water and bring to the boil. Reduce the heat, cover and let it simmer for 30 minutes. Don't stir! Pour the mixture into a jelly bag or sieve lined with fine muslin and drain for 2–3 hours.

Put the liquid and sugar into a pan and simmer, uncovered, skimming off any scum, for about 5 minutes. Pour into warmed, sterilized bottles and leave to cool before sealing. Store in a cool, dark place for 3–6 months.

FRIENDS OVER FOR CHRISTMAS LUNCH

Before and after Christmas Day, all through December, we go to Christmas lunch at work, with our families, sports clubs – any excuse and people will arrange a Christmas lunch, so you end up going to quite a few. Often, more or less the same traditional menu is served. So I have steered away from that; I cook something lighter with the focus on vegetables. It's a time to prepare root vegetables and cabbage in all kinds of festive ways. Then I always do a cured salmon, which is tradition, and in December I use what I call Christmas spices, full of dark, warming flavours. I invite my female friends over, we drink champagne and then the highlight is the cake. There is never a party without cake in my house. We talk about the past year, Christmas, the planning and just how our life is going – a lovely afternoon in the name of hygge.

JUNIPER CURED SALMON

This is an all-time Scandic classic. For years, salmon was very expensive – when I was growing up it was for special occasions only, so was something we ate for Christmas lunch. At the time it was always cured with dill, but I rarely do that now, because I rather love trying it in many different ways, such as in this Christmas version with juniper berries.

SERVES 8

1 tbsp coriander seeds
1 tbsp black peppercorns
50g/1¾oz juniper berries
150g/5¼oz flaky sea salt
200g/1 cup caster
  (granulated) sugar
1 fillet of salmon, about
  1.6kg/3lb 8oz, skin on
Rye Bread, to serve
  (see page 206)
Horseradish cream, to serve

Using a pestle and mortar, lightly crush the coriander seeds and peppercorns together, then tip out into a mixing bowl and lightly crush the juniper berries. Add to the bowl with the salt and sugar and mix well.

Line a ceramic dish at least 40cm/15in long with cling film to overhang the sides, and place the salmon fillet skin-side down in the dish. Now spoon the cure mixture evenly over the salmon, making sure the whole fillet is covered. Wrap the cling film up tightly around the fillet so the mixture stays in place. Refrigerate for 3 days, to cure.

Rinse the cure mixture off with cold water and wipe the fish clean. To serve, cut into slices, leaving the skin behind, and eat with rye bread and horseradish cream.

KALE AND PANCETTA TART

I know that kale these days has become a trendy superfood, but I started cooking with it a long time ago, and it has a long history in Danish food culture. It's a winter food staple usually served in soups and in sauces, with either salted or braised pork. These are very heavy dishes, so I prefer to use kale in vegetables stews and salads – or in a tart, as I have here.

SERVES 8

For the pastry

100g/1 scant cup wholegrain stoneground spelt flour, plus extra for dusting
100g/¾ cup plain (all-purpose) flour
1 tsp sea salt
100g/7 Tbsp butter, diced, plus extra for greasing
100g/3½oz skyr (quark) or fromage frais

For the filling

150g/5¼oz pancetta
300g/10½oz boiled, peeled potatoes
150g/5¼oz kale
1 Tbsp extra virgin olive oil
1 shallot, chopped
3 garlic cloves, chopped
75g/2½oz Cheddar cheese, grated
100g/3½oz crème fraîche or skyr (quark)
4 large eggs, beaten
Freshly grated nutmeg
Sea salt and freshly ground black pepper

Begin with the pastry. Mix both flours and the salt together in a large bowl, then rub in the butter with your fingertips. When it feels like breadcrumbs, mix in the skyr (quark) or fromage frais and knead lightly with your hands just until the ingredients come together into a dough. (Alternatively, just put everything in a food processor and pulse-blend it together.) In both cases, if the dough does not come together, sprinkle in a little water.

Butter a tart tin, about 28cm/11in in diameter, then roll out the dough on a floured surface until big enough to line the tin. Line the tin and put the pastry case in the fridge to rest for 1 hour. Preheat the oven to 180°C/350°F/gas mark 4.

Line the pastry case with baking parchment and fill with baking beans or uncooked rice. Bake in the hot oven for 15 minutes, then remove the beans and parchment and bake for 5 minutes more.

While the case is baking, start to make the filling. Cut the pancetta into cubes and fry in a large, dry sauté pan until golden brown, then take off the heat and set aside. Cut the potatoes into 1-cm/½-in cubes, and rinse and roughly chop the kale. Place the pancetta pan over the heat again, and add the olive oil, shallot and garlic. Let them cook for a few minutes, then add the potatoes and kale and sauté for about 5 minutes. Remove from the heat and set aside for 5 minutes. Now add the grated cheese and crème fraîche, fold in the beaten eggs and season with salt, pepper and nutmeg.

Pour the mixture into the blind-baked pastry case, return to the oven and bake for 30–35 minutes, or until the filling has set but retains a slight wobble.

CHICORY WITH RED ONION AND GRAPEFRUIT

Chicory, or endive, is called *julesalat* in Danish, which means Christmas salad. So, when growing up, I only ever had this as a Christmas salad, and always a Waldorf-style salad. I love the sweet-bitter flavour that chicory has when fried.

SERVES 8

2 small red onions
1 Tbsp olive oil
½ Tbsp sugar
30g/2 Tbsp butter
8 chicory (endives),
 quartered lengthways
2 pink grapefruits
1 bunch of chervil
Sea salt and freshly ground
 black pepper

Preheat the oven to 180°C/350°F/gas mark 4.

Cut the red onion into wedges and gently mix with the olive oil, sugar, and some salt and pepper. Spread out on baking sheet lined with baking parchment and bake in the oven for about 10 minutes. Melt the butter in a frying pan, add the chicory (endive) quarters and fry until golden brown on all sides. Place on a serving dish.

Peel the grapefruits then release the segments from their membranes, working over a bowl to catch the juices, and squeezing out the empty membranes. Spread the grapefruit segments over the chicory then pour over the collected juice (you should have 2 Tbsp). Now add the roasted onion wedges, decorate with the chervil and serve.

CHRISTMAS SALADS

There was a time when I'd never had Jerusalem artichokes other than in soup, and it was quite fancy. Now, I simply love these little knolled roots. They are so deliciously raw, crisp and nutty. The leek dish is a real Danish classic: *slikporrer*. Soft-boiled leeks take me back to a time when vegetables tended to be over-cooked, but leeks become really sweet and flavourful this way.

JERUSALEM ARTICHOKE, APPLE AND TARRAGON

SERVES 8

200g/7oz spelt grains
200g/7oz Jerusalem artichokes
2 slices of lemon
200g/7oz apples (a sharp, crisp variety)
1 Tbsp tarragon leaves

For the walnut pesto

50g/1¾oz walnuts
2 tbsp apple cider vinegar
100ml/½ cup walnut oil
1 tsp honey
Sea salt and freshly ground black pepper

Rinse the spelt in cold water, drain, then boil in fresh water with a little salt for about 20 minutes, or until cooked and tender, but still with a bit of a bite. Drain and cool to room temperature.

Peel the Jerusalem artichokes and cut into thin slices, adding them to a bowl of water with the lemon slices added, so they don't turn brown. Add all the ingredients for the walnut pesto to a food processor and blend into a paste.

Core the apple and cut it into slices. Mix them with the other salad ingredients and season to taste with salt and pepper. Toss with the pesto and serve.

STEAMED LEEKS, GOAT CHEESE AND ALMONDS

SERVES 8

8–10 leeks
75g/5 Tbsp butter
75g/½ cup almonds with skin on, chopped
100g/3½oz creamy goat cheese
2 slices of rye bread, toasted and crumbled
Sea salt and freshly ground black pepper
Chervil, to decorate

Rinse the leeks and trim off both ends, but as little as possible so that the layers stay attached at the root and you keep the dark green at the other end too, which tastes marvellous. Place in a big sauté pan, pour in enough water to come halfway up the leeks, sprinkle with salt and pepper, cover and steam for 5 minutes or until soft. Remove with a slotted spoon, drain, then place on a dish.

While the leeks are cooking, heat the butter until brown in a frying pan, then add the almonds and toast until golden brown. Dot the goat cheese on top of the leeks and sprinkle over the toasted rye crumbs. Just before serving, spoon the brown butter and almonds over the top, sprinkle with pepper and top with chervil.

FRITTERS AND A COLOURFUL SALAD

These small fritters, patties, or whatever you like to call them, are true party stoppers. Every time I serve them people say, "Oh... please can I have the recipe?" I love it that something so simple and low cost can be so delicious.

This salad is made with some of my favourite winter vegetables. I never get tired of cabbage, and could eat it every day. These kinds of hardy vegetables are a really good match for heavy winter food that is high in fat.

CELERIAC FRITTERS

SERVES 8

250g/9oz celeriac
250g/9oz parsley root
2 eggs, lightly beaten
50g/1¾oz sesame seeds
1 green chilli, finely chopped
1 small onion, finely grated
Olive oil, for frying
Sea salt and freshly ground black pepper

Peel the celeriac and parsley root, then grate them both. Mix with all the remaining ingredients in a bowl, seasoning with salt and pepper.

Heat a little oil in a frying pan and, when hot, place spoonfuls of the mixture in the pan and cook for 4–5 minutes on each side, until golden and crisp.

TIP
If you can't get hold of parsley root, these fritters can be made with celeriac alone.

RED CABBAGE, KALE AND POMEGRANATE SALAD

SERVES 8

1 pomegranate
200g/7oz red cabbage
100g/3½oz kale
Sea salt and freshly ground black pepper

For the dressing
2 Tbsp lime juice
3 Tbsp grapeseed oil
1 tsp honey

Cut the pomegranate in half over a bowl lined with a sieve to catch the juices. Take out the seeds and reserve 2 Tbsp of the juices collected for the dressing; set aside.

Thinly slice the cabbage and roughly chop the kale. Mix the cabbage, kale and pomegranate seeds together in a bowl.

For the dressing, mix the 2 Tbsp pomegranate juice with the lime juice, grapeseed oil and honey, with salt and pepper to taste. Just before serving, toss the salad in the dressing, seasoning with salt and pepper.

MY YULE LOG

This pudding is heavenly and takes a bit of work. It's not difficult, but please do read the recipe through carefully before you start. Personally, I love a project like this and I always make the cake part the day before and then decorate with the ganache on the day of serving.

SERVES 8

For the croquant cream
150g/generous ¾ cup caster (superfine) sugar
350g/12oz mascarpone
6 tbsp double (heavy) cream
4 Tbsp icing (confectioners') sugar
1 vanilla pod (bean), split in half lengthways and seeds scraped out

For the sponge
Butter, for greasing
6 egg yolks and 5 egg whites
175g/1 cup caster (granulated) sugar
50g/½ cup cocoa powder, plus extra for dusting
Pinch of salt

For the ganache
170g/6oz dark chocolate (minimum 60% cocoa solids), broken into pieces
2 Tbsp butter, in pieces
150ml/⅔ cup single (light) cream

To decorate
200g/7oz marzipan
Edible gold dust

To make a caramel for the croquant cream, add the sugar to a dry pan and let it melt gently over a medium heat. Stir gently until golden brown, but take care not to let it turn dark brown or it will have a bitter taste. Pour the caramel onto a sheet of baking parchment and leave to harden.

Mix the mascarpone, cream, icing (confectioners') sugar and vanilla seeds. Wrap the hard caramel in a tea towel and break it up with a rolling pin until it has the texture of tiny oats. Fold into the mascarpone mixture and refrigerate. Preheat the oven to 180°C/350°F/gas mark 4 and line a 25 x 35-cm/10 x 14-in baking tin with baking parchment. Butter the parchment.

For the sponge, whisk the egg whites until stiff, then whisk in half the sugar, a little at a time, until it is all incorporated and the mixture is a shiny, stiff meringue. Whisk the egg yolks in a separate, large bowl with the remaining sugar until fluffy and pale, then sift in the cocoa powder and salt. Fold the meringue into the egg yolk mixture then spread gently and evenly into the lined tin. Bake for 10 minutes then remove from the oven and leave to cool for 5 minutes. Place a clean piece of baking parchment on the work surface, dust with cocoa powder and invert the baking tin onto it. Carefully lift off the tin and peel off the baking parchment.

Spread the croquant cream over the sponge and roll it up from one long side, using the cocoa-dusted parchment underneath to help you and to keep the roll very tight, which is essential. With the parchment still wrapped tightly around it, refrigerate for at least 2 hours, or overnight.

To make the ganache, put the chocolate and butter into a heatproof bowl over a pan of simmering water, making sure the bowl is not touching the water. Melt, then remove the bowl from the pan, add the cream and stir until well combined and spreadable. Spread the ganache over the Yule log, then drag a fork lightly through it, so it resembles a little log.

Roll out the marzipan to a 2–3-mm/⅛-in thickness then, using a small knife or a leaf-shaped cookie cutter if you have one, cut out leaves. Press them gently onto the cake and, last but not least, sprinkle with gold dust.

THE BREADS
I BAKE

It is a small miracle that when you combine flour, water, salt and air you produce a loaf of bread, and when human beings found a way to store grains and turn it into flour, the course of history changed. It enabled economies and populations to grow. Bread is in so many ways at the core of our history. Bread is culture, and it is about people. It's also about love. Think about how we all bake for people we love, when we have something to celebrate or when we just want to make sure that we feed our families on proper bread.

I bake bread according to what I am going to eat, and what kind of flour I have in the house. My husband bakes rye bread once a week, which is our staple, everyday bread – often for both breakfast and lunch. I like to eat dense bread with a lot of fibre, like rye bread. I like to bake with different flours such as rye, spelt, oats, einkorn and various heritage grains. I also like buns with nuts and raisins and sweet bread for afternoon tea or a snack. I often think about how bread can be part of our meals at home. I like to have crispbread in my cupboard and I serve it with a light dinner, such as salad and cured salmon. I use leftover bread for cakes, in salads and in soup. It would be impossible to imagine life without bread.

Making bread is also about creating space for hygge at home: the rhythm the bread baking gives to the kitchen and the household. You make the dough, you wait, you pay attention, you bake, then the house transforms into something very homey that you recognize as the fragrance of bread spreads through the house, and then you eat and enjoy the moment.

RYE BREAD

Making rye bread needs some planning, as you have to start by making a sourdough starter. Read the whole recipe carefully before you start.

MAKES 1 LARGE LOAF

For the rye sourdough starter
300ml/1¼ cups buttermilk
300g/2⅔ cups wholegrain stoneground rye flour

Day 1
Sourdough starter from above
850ml/3½ cups lukewarm water
15g/½oz sea salt
750g/6½ cups wholegrain stoneground rye flour

Day 2
500g/1lb 2oz cracked rye
250ml/1 cup cold water
A little oil for the tin

To make the rye sourdough starter, mix the buttermilk and rye flour well in a bowl, cover and leave at room temperature for 3 days. It's important that it doesn't develop mould, but starts bubbling, and a temperature of 23–25°C/73–77°F is ideal for this.

DAY 1
If making your first loaf from the starter, dissolve all the starter in the lukewarm water in a large mixing bowl (for the next loaf use just 3 Tbsp of the starter; the whole quantity of starter is just for the first attempt, and the loaf will be a little bigger). Stir in the salt and rye flour, cover the bowl with a tea towel and leave at room temperature for 12–24 hours. After you have taken out the 3 Tbsp for the next rye bread you are going to make, this starter does not need taking care of. Just let it rest in the refrigerator until next time you need it.

DAY 2
Add the cracked rye and cold water to the dough mixture and stir with a wooden spoon until smooth. It will be too runny to knead. Remove 3 Tbsp of the mixture to an airtight container and refrigerate; this will become your sourdough starter for the next loaf you make (it will need to rest for at least 3 days before you use it, and will last up to 8 weeks).

Lightly oil a large loaf tin, about 30 x 10cm/12 x 4in and 10cm/4in deep. Pour in the dough, cover with a damp tea towel and leave to rise for 3–6 hours, or until the dough has almost reached the top of the tin.

When ready to bake, preheat the oven to 180°C/350°F/gas mark 4. Bake the loaf for 1 hour 45 minutes then immediately turn the loaf out of the tin onto a wire rack to cool. This is great to eat just out of the oven, but as it's difficult to cut, it's better the next day… if you can wait!

SWEET RYE ROLLS

In Scandinavia we eat a lot of bread with spices. Apart from cardamom in almost all soft sweet white bread, we also bake sweet rye bread with green anise. Called *limpa*, it's very common in Sweden, and when I go there I love going to a bakery to buy this distinctive tasting bread. I have been inspired by the flavours for years, and I bake different rolls and breads similar to the limpa bread.

MAKES 24

Day 1
20g/¾oz fresh yeast
300ml/1¼ cups lukewarm water
125g/scant 1 cup strong wholemeal bread flour

Day 2
600g/4⅓ cups strong white bread flour, plus extra for dusting
200g/1¾ cups wholegrain stoneground rye flour
50g/3½ Tbsp butter
10g/⅓oz sea salt
10g/⅓oz anise seeds
50g/1¾oz fresh yeast
350ml/1½ cups lukewarm water
150g/5¼oz dark syrup (available from Scandinavian food sites, or replace with golden [corn] syrup if necessary)
150g/1⅔ cups walnut halves
150g/1 cup dark raisins
1 egg, lightly beaten
50ml/scant ¼ cup cold coffee

DAY 1
Crumble the yeast into the lukewarm water in a bowl and stir to dissolve. Mix in the wholemeal flour, cover with foil and leave overnight.

DAY 2
The next day, mix the white and rye flours together in a bowl. Cut the butter into small cubes and rub it into the flours with your fingertips until it resembles crumbs. Add the salt. Roughly pound the anise seeds using a pestle and mortar, then add these as well.

In another bowl, crumble the yeast into the lukewarm water, then stir in the treacle and the flour and yeast mixture from the day before. Now mix this into the flour and butter mixture. Roughly chop the walnuts and add them to the bowl, with the raisins, and form into a smooth dough. Knead on a floured surface for 5 minutes.

Place in a big bowl, cover with cling film and leave to rise for 2 hours. Knead lightly again and form into 24 rolls. Place on baking sheets lined with baking parchment, cover with tea towels and leave to rise for 30 minutes. Meanwhile, preheat the oven to 200°C/400°F/gas mark 6.

Mix the egg with the coffee. Brush the rolls with some of the egg mixture. Spray cold water in the oven to create steam and bake for 5 minutes, then brush the loaves again with the coffee-egg wash, and bake for another 25–30 minutes. Leave to cool on a wire rack.

EASY MORNING SPELT ROLLS

These rolls are really easy to make, and the dough more or less takes care of itself. Spelt contains gluten, but the gluten structures are weaker so spelt bread does not always rise as much. But don't worry, it still tastes great. I serve these spelt rolls in the morning, or with soup at night.

MAKES 14

10g/⅓oz fresh yeast
700ml/3 cups cold water
400g/2¾ cups fine spelt
  flour, plus extra for dusting
350g/2⅔ cups wholegrain
  spelt flour
50g/1¾oz spelt flakes
5g/1 tsp sea salt

DAY 1

Dissolve the yeast in the water in a bowl, add both flours, the spelt flakes and the salt, mix well for about 10 minutes, then cover and refrigerate overnight.

DAY 2

Preheat the oven to 230°C/450°F/gas mark 8.

Place the dough on a floured work surface and knead lightly. Form into 14 rolls and place on a baking sheet lined with baking parchment. Spray some cold water in the oven to create steam, then bake the rolls for 10 minutes. Now turn down the oven temperature to 200°C/400°F/gas mark 6 and bake for another 10–15 minutes. Leave to cool on a wire rack before eating.

FIVE-GRAIN BREAD

Wholegrains are superfoods because of all the fibre and vitamins they contain, and they are vital for us. But healthy food has to be delicious as well or we won't eat it, so it won't benefit us. I love this bread; it's tasty, has a great texture because of all the grains and also stays moist for a long time.

MAKES 1 LARGE ROUND LOAF

75g/2½oz whole barley grains
75g/2½oz whole rye grains
600ml/2½ cups water
10g/⅓oz fresh yeast
300g/10½oz strong white bread flour, plus extra for dusting
100g/3½oz wholegrain spelt flour
100g/3½oz jumbo oats, plus extra for sprinkling
30g/1oz linseeds (flaxseeds)
10g/⅓oz sea salt
20g/¾oz spelt flakes

Boil the barley and rye grains in the water for about 20 minutes until cooked, then strain, saving the cooking water. Measure the cooking water and add fresh water to top it up to 600ml/2½ cups again.

When the grains and water have cooled to lukewarm, mix the yeast into the water in a mixing bowl, then add the boiled grains, both flours, oats, linseeds (flaxseeds) and salt and mix well with a wooden spoon. Leave to rest for 5 minutes, stir well again and leave for another 5 minutes, then stir again, cover with cling film and refrigerate overnight.

The next day, place the dough on a floured surface and knead just lightly (the dough will be sticky). Line a 25-cm/10-in proving basket with a tea towel and sprinkle the spelt flakes inside. Form a large round bread, place in the proving basket, cover with a tea towel and leave to rise for about 1 hour, or until the dough has risen to the rim of the basket. When nearly ready to bake, preheat the oven to 230°C/450°F/gas mark 8.

Turn the dough out of the proving basket onto a baking sheet lined with baking parchment. Sprinkle with oats and bake in the hot oven for 15 minutes, then turn down the oven temperature to 200°C/400°F/gas mark 6 and bake for another 45 minutes. Transfer to a wire rack to cool before slicing.

FLUTES

Flutes are a kind of Danish baguette, which were very popular in the 1970s with the rise in popularity of French food, and I often baked them when I was young. Usually for get-togethers or parties, it was flute, salad, tart and cheese. This is an old baking recipe of mine that I still use.

MAKES 2

Day 1: first stage
10g/⅓oz fresh yeast
250ml/1 cup lukewarm water
200g/1½ cups strong white
  bread flour, plus extra for
  dusting

Day 1: second stage
250ml/1 cup cold water
300g/2 cups strong white
  bread flour
10g/⅓oz sea salt

DAY 1
First, dissolve the yeast in the lukewarm water in a large bowl, then add the flour and mix well. Cover the bowl with a clean tea towel and leave at room temperature for 3–4 hours. Add the cold water, flour and salt and mix well. Cover the bowl with cling film and refrigerate overnight.

DAY 2
Preheat the oven to 220°C/425°F/gas mark 7.

Place the dough on a floured work surface and leave to rest for 30 minutes. Knead it lightly, divide in half and form each half into a long, thin flute. Place on a baking sheet lined with baking parchment and slash the tops diagonally at intervals, using a razor or very sharp knife. Brush with water.

Bake in the oven for 20 minutes, then check if the flutes are done. If not, bake for another 5 minutes, then leave to cool on a wire rack.

EINKORN BREAD

Over the last 30 years many different kinds of grains have emerged. For somebody like me, who loves baking, this is so exciting because it offers so many opportunities for working with new flavours and textures. This is a great bread for sandwiches, or toast for breakfast during the week. I like toasted bread with avocado and chilli flakes.

MAKES 1 LOAF

500ml/2 cups buttermilk
500ml/2 cups cold water
40g/1½oz fresh yeast
20g/¾oz honey
50ml/scant ¼ cup extra
  virgin olive oil
700g/1lb 8½oz einkorn flour
300g/2 cups strong white
  bread flour
30g/1oz sea salt
Butter, for greasing

Mix the buttermilk, water and yeast together in a bowl, then add the honey and olive oil. Mix both flours with the salt in a separate bowl, then add the dry ingredients to the yeast mixture, and mix really well, using a wooden spoon or a mixer. Keep mixing until the dough starts turning stringy and leaving the sides of the bowl. If you do it by hand, it's OK to take breaks, but it's important to give it a really good mix.

Leave to rise in the bowl at room temperature for 30 minutes, then punch down the dough and stir again with a wooden spoon. Transfer to a 2-litre buttered loaf tin and leave to rise at room temperature for about 2 hours.

Preheat the oven to 220°C/425°F/gas mark 7. Bake the loaf for 30–35 minutes, then turn out onto a wire rack to cool.

SPELT FOCACCIA

This is a bread with many purposes: served with food, it's great if you have lots of people over for dinner. It's also perfect for sandwiches or for a pre-dinner snack with olive oil. It keeps well and is quite moist for a day – true focaccia from Liguria is made with potato, as this one is. It's good to share whole when sitting around the table; you just tear it up and eat with butter.

MAKES 1 LARGE FOCACCIA

250g/9oz potatoes, peeled
45g/1½oz fresh yeast
250ml/1 cup lukewarm milk
50ml/scant ¼ cup extra
  virgin olive oil
2 eggs, beaten
1 Tbsp caster (granulated)
  sugar
325g/2½ cups wholegrain
  spelt flour
600g/4½ cups strong white
  bread flour
1 tsp sea salt

For the top
50ml/¼ cup olive oil
20g/¾oz coarse sea salt
Leaves from 4–5 rosemary
  sprigs

First, cook the potatoes in plenty of boiling, salted water and reserve 250ml/1 cup of the cooking water when you drain them. Finely purée the potatoes and leave the cooking water to cool to lukewarm.

Dissolve the yeast in the milk then add the reserved potato cooking water and the puréed potatoes, olive oil, eggs and sugar; mix well. Now add both flours and the salt and mix very well. Cover the bowl with a tea towel and leave to rise for 2 hours.

Line a roasting tin, 30 x 40cm/12 x 16in, with baking parchment. Tip the dough gently into the tin, stretching it out until it fits the tin. Cover with a tea towel and leave to rise for 2 hours.

Preheat the oven to 200°C/400°F/gas mark 6 and place a heatproof bowl filled with water in the base of the oven, to create steam. Using your thumb, make indentations in the dough at intervals. Brush the dough with the olive oil and sprinkle with the sea salt and rosemary leaves. Bake in the oven for 30 minutes, then remove from the oven and gently transfer the focaccia from the roasting tin to a wire rack to cool.

CRISPBREAD

Quintessentially Scandinavian and famous around the world, crispbread can now be found in supermarkets everywhere. But I will say this: nothing beats the home-baked version, it's just so much tastier.

MAKES 15 PIECES

50g/1¾oz fresh yeast
500ml/2 cups lukewarm
   water
100g/7 Tbsp butter
500g/4⅓ cups wholegrain
   stoneground rye flour,
   plus extra for dusting
200g/1½ cups strong white
   bread flour
1 tsp sea salt
1 tsp caster (granulated)
   sugar
1 Tbsp caraway seeds,
   lightly crushed

To spread

200g/¾ cup soft goat cheese
3 Tbsp natural yogurt
4 Tbsp chopped chives
Sea salt and freshly ground
   black pepper

First, dissolve the yeast in the warm water in a large bowl. Add the butter, both flours, salt, sugar and caraway seeds and mix together. Leave to rise for 1 hour 30 minutes.

Preheat the oven to 245°C/475°F/gas mark 9. Place the dough on a floured surface and divide into 15 small balls. Roll out each ball into a very thin, flat pancake and prick the surface all over with a fork. Working in batches, place on a baking sheet lined with baking parchment and bake for 8–10 minutes, then repeat until all the dough is used. Cool on a wire rack and store in an airtight container for 2–3 weeks.

Mix the goat cheese, yogurt, chives and salt and pepper to make the perfect spread for these crispbreads.

SKORPER

These are weird little dry things, kind of a savoury biscotti that we like to make and keep in tins, then eat for breakfast, lunch and snacks. I like them best with salmon and cream cheese – an all-time Scandinavian classic.

MAKES 24

Day 1
25g/1oz fresh yeast
300ml/1¼ cups buttermilk
100g/scant 1 cup wholegrain
   stoneground rye flour

Day 2
25g/1oz fresh yeast
200ml/¾ cup water
50ml/scant ¼ cup golden
   (corn) syrup
150g/⅔ cup cold butter
200g/1¾ cups wholegrain
   stoneground rye flour
300g/2¼ cups strong white
   bread flour
10g/⅓oz sea salt
100g/3½oz rye flakes
1 tsp each of fennel seeds,
   anise seeds and caraway
   seeds, lightly crushed

DAY 1
Mix the yeast, buttermilk and rye flour together in a small bowl, cover with a tea towel and leave overnight at room temperature.

DAY 2
Add the yeast and water to the overnight starter mixture with the syrup. Cut the butter into cubes. Mix the flours in a bowl and crumble in the butter, mixing with your fingers until it resembles breadcrumbs. Add the salt, rye flakes and crushed seeds, then add the starter mixture and mix to a firm dough. Cover and leave to rise for 1 hour, then form the dough into 24 small oval rolls and place them on baking sheets lined with baking parchment. Cover with tea towels and leave to rise for 40 minutes.

Preheat the oven to 200°C/400°F/gas mark 6. Bake for 15 minutes, then transfer to a wire rack to cool and reduce the oven temperature to 150°C/300°F/gas mark 2. When cool, split each skorper in half with a knife, and place the halves back on the baking sheets. Bake in the oven for 25 minutes, then leave to cool before eating. Stored in an airtight container, they will keep for weeks.

SOURDOUGH BREAD

Sourdough is not easy to do at home, and it takes commitment to keep your sourdough going because it needs to be fed every day. There is no guarantee that sourdough bread will turn out great each time, but that is also the beauty of it: it's a piece of nature in the kitchen. It behaves differently every time. I do not recommend making sourdough bread if you are not a patient person. It takes practice, and you need to make space and time for it.

MAKES 1 LOAF

For the sourdough biga/leaven

150g/1 cup strong white bread flour
100g/¾ cup strong wholemeal bread flour
300ml/1¼ cups water

NOTE: Ideally you should feed the biga every day, but if you forget for a few days, just discard 80% and refill as though there had been no gap. Mine has worked for years despite me sometimes forgetting. But I do get people to babysit my biga when I travel!

For the bread

150g/5¼oz sourdough biga/leaven, from above
350ml/1½ cups water
400g/3 cups strong white bread flour, plus extra for dusting
100g/¾ cup strong wholemeal bread flour
8g/¼oz sea salt

FOR THE SOURDOUGH BIGA/LEAVEN

Put both flours into a large mixing bowl. Gradually pour in the water, mixing with your hand or a balloon whisk until it has the consistency of pancake batter. Cover with a plate or similar and leave overnight. The next day, discard 80% of the mixture and top it up with the same ratio of flours and water to make up for the amount discarded. Mix well. Do this for 5–10 days until it comes to life: you will notice small bubbles, or a sour smell, and then it's ready.

FOR THE BREAD

Mix the 150g/5¼oz biga/leaven with 300ml/1¼ cups of the water and both flours and set aside to rest for 30 minutes. Then add the remaining 50ml/¼ cup water and the salt, mix really well again and knead the dough in the bowl. Leave to rise for 3–6 hours, punching it down now and then and giving the dough a turn.

Take the dough out onto a floured surface and form it into a round loaf. Line a proving basket 25cm/10in in diameter with a clean tea towel and dust with flour. Add the formed dough to the basket, cover with a tea towel and leave for 45 minutes to 1 hour until the dough has more or less risen to the rim of the basket.

Preheat the oven to 250°C/475°F/gas mark 9 and place a heatproof bowl filled with water in the base of the oven, to create steam (or you can toss some cold water into the oven as you put the bread in). Gently turn the risen dough out onto either a baking sheet lined with baking parchment or place the dough on a large baking or pizza stone using a wide, wooden pizza spatula. Slash the top of the loaf to make a cross using a razor or very sharp knife. Bake for 45–55 minutes, turning down the temperature after 15 minutes to 220°C/425°F/gas mark 7. Leave to cool on a wire rack.

CHRISTMAS DINNER AT MY HOUSE

Christmas dinner is something I look forward to every year. I spend days brooding over my recipes and planning my days. Christmas dinner is about family traditions combined with new rituals you've created. Most of my Christmas recipes come from my grandmother and mother.

In Denmark, Christmas celebrations take place on the evening of 24th December. We start at 6pm with a glass of champagne and follow with dinner at 7pm. It's true hygge, and an evening that I love. After dinner we dance around the Christmas tree and sing carols, which in my family is not taken as seriously as I would like. After dinner and dancing it's finally time to open the presents.

Here are the recipes for my Christmas dinner with a selection of salads that I think a dream match for roasted duck. As we say in Danish: *God jul!*

ROAST DUCK

Roasting duck is a welcome event for me every Christmas; it is a part of my menu that never changes. It would not be Christmas without roast duck, always organic from a small farm on Fyn island. I either slow roast it or barbecue it and I always make the same stuffing. Cooking duck is not difficult – just make sure it is good quality and then keep an eye on it and check on it often while it is cooking.

SERVES 8 FOR CHRISTMAS EVE

2 ducks, each about 3.5kg/
   7lb 12oz
Sea salt and freshly ground
   black pepper

For the stuffing

2 Cox's orange apples
2 shallots, sliced
200g/7oz prunes
10 thyme sprigs, leaves only
10g/⅓oz coarse sea salt
1 Tbsp freshly ground black
   pepper

Duck stock

2 carrots
200g/7oz celeriac
2 onions
2 duck legs
1 bottle of red wine
1.5 litres/6 cups water
1 Tbsp black peppercorns
4 bay leaves
1 Tbsp coarse sea salt

Preheat the oven to 120°C/250°F/gas mark ½.

Remove the giblets from the ducks and rinse them inside and out. If there is too much fat inside, remove some of it, then you can melt it and save to use for crisp roast potatoes. For the stuffing, cut the apples into 2-cm/¾-in chunks. Mix all the stuffing ingredients together and use to stuff the birds. Close the ducks with meat needles and rub the outsides in salt and pepper. Place breast-side down on a wire rack set over a roasting tin and transfer to the oven for 2 hours.

After 2 hours, turn the duck around, breast-side up, and roast for another 3–4 hours. Check the temperature where the meat meets the bone at the thighs using a meat thermometer – it should be 68°C/154°F. When they are ready, take the ducks out of the oven, leave to rest for 5–10 minutes and joint each one into 8–12 pieces.

DUCK STOCK

Peel the carrots, celeriac and onions and cut into chunks. Brown the duck legs in a large saucepan in their own fat, turning occasionally until golden brown. Add all the other ingredients and bring to the boil, then reduce the heat and let it simmer, uncovered, for 2–3 hours. Strain through a sieve, leave to cool and store in the fridge. When cold, you can easily scrape off the fat that sets on top (save it in a jar for cooking). There should be about 1 litre/4 cups stock. It can be kept in the freezer, and therefore be made well ahead of using it.

CARAMEL POTATOES AND GRAVY

Caramel potatoes are the best, and also maybe the weirdest. You either love them or hate them, and in my family we love them. The secret to perfecting them is patience. After you have added the potatoes you slowly and very gently turn them around so the caramel coats the potatoes layer by layer until they are golden brown and sticky.

Making gravy is a bit like getting dressed in winter, it's about adding layer upon layer: you little by little add salt, port, pepper, redcurrant jelly and cream until you think it is perfect. The gravy makes the whole Christmas meal come together.

CARAMEL POTATOES

SERVES 8

2kg/4lb 6oz small potatoes
300g/1⅔ cups caster (granulated) sugar
175g/¾ cup salted butter
Pinch of sea salt

Cook the potatoes in boiling, salted water until tender. It is important that you do not overcook them – keep them firm. Drain them, peel and leave to cool (this is best done the day before). Place the peeled potatoes in a colander, pour cold water over them and leave to drain well.

Melt the sugar over a medium heat in a large, heavy-based saucepan. Don't stir it! When the sugar is melted and golden brown like caramel, add the butter and let the mixture simmer until it becomes smooth, stirring as little as possible. Add the potatoes and gently turn them in the caramel. Cook over a low heat for 30–40 minutes, turning regularly so the caramel coats the potatoes layer by layer; serve hot.

GRAVY

SERVES 8

About 1 litre/4 cups Duck Stock
  (see page 228)
75g/5 Tbsp salted butter
6 Tbsp plain (all-purpose) flour
100ml/scant ½ cup port
1 tsp Danish Blue cheese
1 Tbsp redcurrant jelly
300ml/1¼ cups double (heavy) cream
A dash of balsamic vinegar
1 tsp gravy browning (optional)

For the gravy, heat the Duck Stock in a pan. Melt the butter in a separate pan, whisk in the flour and cook until even and shiny, with absolutely no lumps. Add the hot stock little by little, stirring after each addition until all the stock is used. Slowly bring to the boil then add the port, blue cheese, redcurrant jelly, cream, balsamic vinegar and some pepper, stirring constantly. Leave to simmer for a few minutes, season to taste with salt, and some more pepper. Add the gravy browning, if you want a darker colour. Reheat when ready to serve.

BUTTERNUT SQUASH SALAD

Vegetables have always been a big part of my daily diet – I just love them – so Christmas and other holidays can be hard for me, because there is so much meat and fat involved. I find that if I include a lot of vegetables I feel so much better, so my Christmas dinner has a lot of salads and vegetable combinations.

SERVES 8

1 butternut squash,
  about 500g/1lb 2oz
3 Tbsp olive oil
1 tsp Szechuan peppercorns,
  crushed with a pestle and
  mortar
½ red cabbage, about
  500g/1lb 2oz
Sea salt and freshly ground
  black pepper
1 bunch of coriander
  (cilantro), to serve

For the dressing
1 Tbsp grapeseed oil
3 Tbsp soy sauce
Sea salt and freshly ground
  black pepper

Preheat the oven to 180°C/350°F/gas mark 4.

Cut the squash in half lengthways, remove all the seeds and cut across into thin slices, 5mm/¼in thick, with the peel still on. Spread out on a baking sheet lined with baking parchment, mix with the olive oil, Szechuan pepper and some salt and bake for 10 minutes, then leave to cool on the sheet.

While the squash is in the oven, cut the red cabbage into slices about 5mm/¼in thick, rinse in cold water and drain well.

Mix the dressing ingredients together, and just before serving mix the butternut, red cabbage and dressing together, place on a serving dish and decorate with coriander (cilantro).

CHRISTMAS COLESLAW

To make the Christmas dinner complete, cabbage of some sort is a must. Instead of cooked red cabbage, as an alternative you can serve raw sprout salad which will lighten up the meal a little.

SERVES 8

1 pomegranate
200g/7oz Brussels sprouts
100g/3½oz celery
50g/1¾oz kale
50g/1¾oz walnuts, chopped
Sea salt and freshly ground
   black pepper

For the dressing
2 Tbsp lemon juice
1 Tbsp Dijon mustard
1 Tbsp honey
1 Tbsp hazelnut oil

Cut the pomegranate in half and, working over a bowl lined with a sieve to catch the juices, remove the seeds and transfer to a big mixing bowl. Cut the sprouts in half then cut into thin slices. Thinly slice the celery and finely chop the kale. Chop the walnuts, then add everything to the bowl with the pomegranate seeds and mix.

For the dressing, add the lemon juice to the pomegranate juices, with the mustard and honey, then slowly add the oil and mix to a smooth dressing. Just before serving, mix the salad with the dressing and season to taste with salt and pepper.

TURNIPS AND APPLES WITH THYME

Turnips and apples really suit each other and they go so well with duck. They're also great the next day for a feast of leftovers, just on rye bread.

SERVES 8

3 Cox's orange apples
500g/1lb 2oz turnips
30g/2 Tbsp butter
10 thyme sprigs
2–3 Tbsp apple cider vineagr
Sea salt and freshly ground
   black pepper

Cut the apples and turnips into wedges about 1cm/½in wide. Melt the butter in a large frying pan, add the turnips and thyme and sauté for 5 minutes or until golden, then lower the heat and add the apples with some salt and pepper. Sprinkle in the vinegar and gently stir the apples and turnips around.

Cook for about 5 minutes more, season to taste with salt and pepper and serve right away.

COLD RICE PUDDING
WITH WARM CHERRY SAUCE

I have many rituals over Christmas – as lots of us have, I guess – and hygge is a big part of these. Apart from being the ultimate pudding and a Christmas classic in most households in Denmark, this rice pudding, or *risalamande*, is also like a wrap-up thing for me. I love – late on 24th December, when Christmas Eve is over and everybody is in bed or has gone home – to get up, light a few candles, cuddle up in the sofa and treat myself to a big portion of rice pudding. I just sit and enjoy this moment of bliss. When we serve the rice pudding, we play a game. A whole almond is hidden in the pudding, and whoever finds it in their bowl receives a present: the "almond gift". You should try to hide the almond if you get it – to keep the suspense going – until the whole bowl has been eaten... but that can be a daunting task!

SERVES 8

2 vanilla pods (beans)
300ml/1¼ cups water
300g/1⅔ cups short-grain
   pudding rice
1.6 litres/7 cups whole milk
2 tsp sea salt
2 Tbsp caster (granulated)
   sugar
150g/1¼ cups blanched
   almonds
500ml/generous 2 cups
   double (heavy) cream

For the cherry sauce
700g/1lb 9oz pitted cherries,
   fresh or frozen
150g/generous ¾ cup caster
   (granulated) sugar, or to
   taste
1 vanilla pod (bean)
500ml/2 cups water
3 Tbsp cornflour (cornstarch)

Split one of the vanilla pods (beans) in half lengthways, without cutting all the way through. Bring the water to the boil in a large, heavy-based pan, then add the rice and let it boil for 2 minutes, stirring. Add the milk and the split vanilla pod, stirring until it returns to the boil. Lower the heat, cover and cook for 15–20 minutes, stirring often so it doesn't catch, until the rice is just cooked (just beyond al dente but not over-cooked). Remove from the heat and add the salt. Cover and set aside for 10 minutes, then stir in the sugar and leave until cold, or overnight.

Remove the vanilla pod and transfer the cold rice mixture to a serving bowl. Set aside 1 whole almond, which must be saved for the game! Roughly chop the rest. Split the second vanilla pod in half lengthways, scrape out the seeds with the tip of a knife and add the seeds to the rice pudding. Whip the cream in a bowl until it forms soft peaks. Fold one-third of the cream into the rice to loosen, then fold in the rest and add the chopped almonds. Taste the pudding: it should be sweet with a flavour of vanilla. Push the whole almond down into the pudding so it is well hidden.

For the cherry sauce, mix the cherries, sugar, vanilla pod and water in a saucepan. Bring to the boil, then reduce the heat and let it simmer for 15 minutes. Dust the cornflour (cornstarch) into 2 Tbsp water in a cup and stir. Slowly add the cornflour paste to the cherries, stirring constantly, until they thicken, and season to taste with more sugar, if you want.

Serve the cold rice pudding with the hot cherry sauce.

S O M E T H I N G
SWEET

Life without cakes would be a bit too sinister. I believe cake is good for you mentally; the pleasure you get from something sweet contributes to your quality of life in a way that I don't think should be disregarded. I don't believe that a piece of cake made from good, organic produce could possibly be bad for you. I do not eat cake every day, but I do often, and I choose my cakes with care. I prefer my own baked ones, or just home-baked cakes in general. I love something a bit fresh and sour, and I like to use rhubarb and berries. Fresh ripe fruit is a favourite of mine for pudding, but can be difficult here in the north, so when berries are in season in July and August, I eat them every day. I have strawberries almost every day with cold milk poured over.

For me cakes are also quite seasonal. I like to eat Rosenbrød (see page 274), a Danish pastry with rose icing, in the summer, whereas Buttermilk Fromage (a little like panna cotta, see page 270) I can eat all year round, just changing the fruit served on top to match the season. Buttermilk Soup (see page 255), however, I would never eat outside the summer months.

In winter, I enjoy cakes made with apples or plums, and Kringle (like a Danish pastry, but the dough isn't laminated – see page 252), or cakes made with dried fruits. I also love Pecan Pie with a Rye Crust (see page 256), which is quite sweet but has an edge to it. For me there is always an occasion to bake a cake and share it with my loved ones.

LEMON MOON CAKE

Imagine 20 years ago, when shops had stricter laws for opening hours. This cake was for when you decided it was time for some hygge, but all the main shops were closed. So you would go to the corner shop, or gas station, and buy a stale cake in plastic wrap called *citronmåne*, or "lemon moon". Police officers and fire fighters in particular are known for sharing this cake in their coffee breaks, because hygge is something we also make time for during working hours. I never cared for this odd factory cake, so I created this recipe for a homemade version instead. It is perfect with a cup of tea on a windy autumn afternoon.

SERVES 8

250g/18 Tbsp butter, plus extra for greasing
200g/1½ cups almonds, skin on
250g/1¼ cups caster (granulated) sugar
4 eggs
150g/1 cup plus 2 Tbsp plain (all-purpose) flour
2 tsp baking powder
About 100ml/scant ½ cup whole milk

For the icing

100g/3½oz fromage blanc
100g/3½oz cream cheese
1 Tbsp finely grated unwaxed lemon zest and 2 Tbsp juice
1 Tbsp icing (confectioners') sugar

Preheat the oven to 180°C/350°F/gas mark 4. Butter a 28-cm/11-in round springform cake tin and line the base with baking parchment.

Blitz the almonds, with their skins, in a food processor until ground as finely as possible. You will get far superior results with freshly ground almonds than using ready ground, so do take the trouble and don't skip this step!

Cream the butter and sugar together using an electric mixer, until light and fluffy. Beat in the eggs one at a time, beating well after each addition. Sift the flour and baking powder and mix them into the ground almonds. Fold this mixture into the creamed mixture, using a spatula, and adding enough of the milk to reach a dropping consistency.

Pour the batter into the prepared tin and bake for 1 hour, or until cooked. Leave to cool on a wire rack.

For the icing, mix the fromage blanc, cream cheese, lemon zest and juice. Stir in the icing (confectioners') sugar until combined. Cut the cooled cake in half to give 2 half moon shapes. Save one half for another time (freezing it is a good idea). Spread the icing over the remaining half moon, and serve with tea.

MERINGUE LAYER CAKE

I think this cake needs no introduction. It's truly a showstopper cake, only for the summertime when strawberries are sweet and tender.

SERVES 8

For the meringue
Butter, for greasing
6 egg whites
300g/1⅔ cups caster
  (superfine) sugar
½ tsp clear vinegar
Pinch of sea salt

For the caramel
100g/generous ½ cup caster
  (granulated) sugar

For the almonds
50g/1¾oz whole almonds
1 tsp honey
1 tbsp balsamic vinegar

For the cream
500ml/2 cups double
  (heavy) cream
1kg/2lb 3oz strawberries,
  hulled and rinsed

Preheat the oven to 110°C/225°F/gas mark ¼. Line a large baking sheet (or 2) with baking parchment and, using a pencil, draw 3 circles, each 17cm/6¾in in diameter. Turn the parchment over on each so the pencil mark is underneath but still visible. Butter inside each circle.

Using an electric mixer, whisk the egg whites until stiff, then whisk in the sugar 1 tbsp at a time, until very stiff and the sugar has all been added. Add the vinegar and salt, then spread the meringue evenly inside the buttered circles. Bake for 1 hour 30 minutes, turn off the heat, open the oven door and leave it ajar for 15 minutes, with the meringues still in the oven. Remove the meringues from the oven and leave to cool on a wire rack, still on their sheets of baking parchment.

While the meringue is in the oven, make the caramel. Add the sugar to a dry pan and let it melt gently over a medium heat; do not stir, just shake the pan gently now and then. When it has turned golden (it is very important is doesn't go too dark brown or it will taste bitter), pour onto a piece of baking parchment and leave to cool and harden.

Once the meringue is cold, put the almonds in a dry frying pan to toast, and as soon as they start to colour add the honey and mix well. Now add the balsamic vinegar, let it boil for a few seconds and stir well. Take off the heat and let the balsamic settle. Place a piece of baking parchment on a tray, spoon the almonds out onto the parchment and leave to cool.

Whip the cream until light and fluffy and quarter the strawberries. Remove the parchment from the meringue bases and place the least attractive disc on a serving plate. Spread over a third of the whipped cream, then place a third of the strawberries on the cream. Add the second meringue disc and repeat the layers twice more. Stand the remaining strawberries in the cream on the top. With wet hands, loosen the almonds from the parchment and use to decorate the cake. Break the caramel into rustic-looking pieces and add to the top. Cut into slices and serve with a chilled glass of Prosecco.

RHUBARB AND CHOCOLATE LAYER CAKE

This is the cake I make when something unexpected happens. I always keep a baked sponge in my freezer, as they defrost very quickly, and I do admit it's a bit crazy always to be prepared to serve cake for people who come to visit unexpectedly. But any visit will be much more hyggeligt with a home-baked cake. If not using a frozen one, bake the cake a day in advance, or it will be too difficult to cut.

SERVES 8

For the sponge
Butter, for greasing
4 large eggs
200g/generous 1 cup caster (granulated) sugar
175g/1½ cups plain (all-purpose) flour
1 tsp baking powder

For the rhubarb cream
1 vanilla pod (bean)
500g/1lb 2oz rhubarb, cut into 1-cm/½-in pieces
150g/generous ¾ cup caster (granulated) sugar
500ml/2 cups double (heavy) cream

For the chocolate icing
200g/7oz dark chocolate (62% cocoa solids)
50g/3½ Tbsp butter
100ml/scant ½ cup single (light) cream

Preheat the oven to 180°C/350°F/gas mark 4. Butter a round 25-cm/10-in cake tin and line the base with baking parchment.

Beat the eggs and sugar together with an electric whisk until light and fluffy; they should double or even triple in volume, and turn pale. Sift over the flour and baking powder and gently fold them in. Pour into the prepared tin and bake in the oven for 25 minutes, until a skewer inserted into the middle emerges clean. Leave in the tin to cool on a wire rack, before removing from the tin. Leave overnight.

The next day, for the rhubarb cream, split the vanilla pod (bean) lengthways and scrape out the seeds with the tip of a knife. Put the rhubarb, sugar and vanilla seeds into a small pan and stir until the sugar has melted. Cook over a gentle heat for 10 minutes, then set aside to cool.

Put the chocolate and butter in a heatproof bowl set over a pan of simmering water, making sure the base of the bowl is not touching the water, and heat until melted. Remove the bowl from the pan and whisk in the cream until it is a spreadable consistency. Cut the sponge across in half and spread the chocolate icing over the top of each half.

Whip the cream and fold it into the rhubarb compote, saving some rhubarb pieces for decoration. Take one chocolate covered sponge and place on a round serving dish and spread with half the rhubarb cream. Place the second iced sponge on top and spread the rest of the rhubarb cream on top. Decorate with the reserved rhubarb.

RHUBARB TRIFLE WITH RYE CRUMBS

Trifle can be made with any berry or fruit in season. When I was growing up, I ate a lot of rhubarb – probably because it was cheap or it grew in my mother's garden, I am not sure. Traditionally in a trifle we use macaroons and double cream, but lately I have started using rye breadcrumbs roasted in a little sugar, and Greek yogurt. It's a wonderful combination, which reminds me of a childhood snack: a piece of rye bread with butter topped with strawberries or bananas. Simple ways of getting sweet treats are what we need, instead of snack bars full of unrecognizable ingredients.

SERVES 4

For the rhubarb
800g/1lb 12oz rhubarb, rinsed
  and cut into 2-cm/¾-in
  pieces
300g/1⅔ cups caster
  (granulated) sugar

For the rye breadcrumbs
25g/scant 2 Tbsp butter
300g/10½oz dry rye bread,
  crumbled by hand
50g/¼ cup caster
  (granulated) sugar

For the yogurt cream
1 vanilla pod (bean)
300ml/1¼ cups Greek yogurt
2 tbsp caster (granulated)
  sugar

4 mint leaves, to serve

Put the rhubarb and sugar in a saucepan and stir until the sugar has melted. Simmer over a gentle heat until the rhubarb has just softened, about 5 minutes.

Melt the butter in a frying pan, add the crumbled bread and sugar and toast over a low heat until crisp.

For the yogurt cream, split the vanilla pod (bean) lengthways and scrape out the seeds with the tip of a knife. Put the vanilla seeds, yogurt and sugar in a bowl and mix well.

Use four glasses to assemble the trifle. Place a layer of rhubarb in the base of each, then a layer of yogurt cream, then toasted crumbs. Repeat once more. Refrigerate until ready to serve, decorated with a mint leaf.

KRINGLE

This is a very classic Danish cake with yeasted dough that we eat for breakfast on special occasions, but also as afternoon cake with coffee. Kringle is always part of the traditional cake table. I have worked on the recipe for years, and I bake it often because my love for Kringle never seems to lessen. The recipe makes three, which serves about 10 people, so I always freeze one of them; it doesn't work so well in a smaller quantity.

MAKES 3

For the kringle

100ml/⅓ cup plus 1 Tbsp
  lukewarm milk
50g/2oz fresh yeast
3 eggs, lightly beaten
100g/½ cup caster
  (granulated) sugar
1 tsp salt
350g/1½ cups butter
550g/4¼ cups '00' flour,
  plus extra for dusting

For the filling

150g/1¼ cups roughly
  chopped almonds
200g/1 cup caster
  (granulated) sugar
250g/18 Tbsp soft butter
150g/1 cup raisins
1 egg, lightly beaten
50g/⅔ cup flaked (slivered)
  almonds

Pour the milk into a bowl, crumble over the yeast and stir to dissolve. Add the eggs, sugar and salt, cover and leave for 30 minutes. Meanwhile, cut the butter into cubes and, with your hands, rub them into the flour. When the 30 minutes are up, mix the yeast mixture into the flour mixture. Knead on a floured surface until you have a smooth dough. The dough is very delicate, so you might have to use a bit more flour and handle it with care. Place in a bowl, cover and leave to rise at room temperature for about 1 hour.

For the filling, mix the chopped almonds into a paste with the sugar and butter. Set aside.

Return to the dough. Roll it out on a floured surface into a rectangle. Fold it into three, crossways, like a business letter, then turn it by 90°. Now divide the dough into 3 and roll each out into a rectangle.

Divide the filling into 3. Spread each portion out over a 4-cm/1½-in wide strip down the middle of each dough rectangle. Scatter the raisins over the filling. Fold the short ends up over the filling and then the long sides, first one side over the filling and then the other, so they overlap by 1cm/⅜in. Place on baking sheets lined with baking parchment, cover with tea towels and let rise again for 30–45 minutes or until the dough feels a bit puffy when you touch it gently.

Preheat the oven to 220°C/425°F/gas mark 7.

Brush each pastry with egg and sprinkle with the flaked almonds. Bake for 15–20 minutes, keeping an eye on them so they don't turn too dark. If they are looking too dark, reduce the oven temperature to 200°C/400°F/ gas mark 6. Cool down on a wire rack and serve warm or cold.

COLD BUTTERMILK SOUP AND KAMMERJUNKER

A classic pudding for long, warm summer days at the beach house. Buttermilk soup was not a pudding when I was growing up – it was supper. I remember what a lovely surprise it was when you were called as a child to leave the water and the beach and come up to the house. Then a bathrobe was swept around you and you sat on the veranda and slurped cold buttermilk soup. I can hear the voices, the sea, and feel the love from my grandmother as we sat there at the table together.

SERVES 8

For the kammerjunker (biscotti)
125g/9 Tbsp butter
100g/generous ½ cup caster (granulated) sugar
1 egg
250g/1¾ cups plus 2 Tbsp plain (all-purpose) flour, plus extra for dusting
1 tsp baking powder
1 tsp ground cardamom
1 Tbsp finely grated unwaxed lemon zest
50ml/scant ¼ cup whole milk

For the buttermilk soup
2 vanilla pods (beans)
4 egg yolks
150g/generous ¾ cup caster (granulated) sugar
1 Tbsp finely grated unwaxed lemon zest and 3 Tbsp juice
2 litres/8½ cups buttermilk

Preheat the oven to 200°C/400°F/gas mark 6.

Start by making the biscotti. Beat the butter and sugar together until light and creamy, then add the egg and beat again. Sift the flour and baking powder into a bowl and add cardamom and lemon zest, then mix into the creamed mixture, together with the milk.

Knead the dough lightly on a floured surface, then roll it into a long, thin sausage. Cut into small even-sized pieces, and use your hands to shape them into balls about the size of walnuts. Place on two baking sheets lined with baking parchment and bake for 7 minutes.

Cut the biscotti in half, before they start to cool down. Place them back on the baking sheets and bake for another 20 minutes, or until golden brown. Transfer to a wire rack to cool, then store in an airtight tin (they will keep for several weeks).

Make the cold soup a few hours before serving. Split the vanilla pods (beans) lengthways and scrape out the seeds with the tip of a knife, into a bowl. Add the egg yolks and sugar and beat together until pale and fluffy. Add the lemon zest and juice, and the buttermilk. Chill for 2–3 hours. To serve, break the biscotti into crumbs with your hands over the soup and eat immediately.

PECAN PIE WITH A RYE CRUST

Many years ago when I was only 19 years old, I travelled to New York to fulfil my childhood dream: to live in the city that never sleeps. One of my first encounters with the American cake culture was pecan pie. I absolutely loved it. The dark flavour from the brown sugar and syrup reminded me of another favourite of mine, the Danish *brunsviger*. I have created my own version of the pecan pie that is very close to the classic, except that the crust is different and uses rye flour, which I think works beautifully.

SERVES 8

For the pastry
100g/¾ cup plain (all-purpose) flour
100g/1 scant cup coarse rye flour
50g/5¾ Tbsp icing (confectioners') sugar
Pinch of coarse sea salt
75g/⅓ cup salted butter, cut into small cubes, plus extra for greasing
75g/⅓ cup skyr (quark) or fromage blanc

For the filling
50g/3½ Tbsp salted butter
200ml/¾ cup golden (corn) syrup
2 large eggs
100g/½ cup dark brown sugar
200g/7oz pecans, coarsely chopped

Whipped cream or vanilla ice cream, to serve

To make the pastry, mix the flours with the icing (confectioners') sugar and salt in a bowl. Add the butter and rub it into the flour mixture until the mixture resembles dry breadcrumbs. Add the skyr (quark) and mix it in to make a dough. (Alternatively, put all the ingredients into a food processor and process to a dough.)

Lightly butter a round tart tin, 28cm/11in in diameter, and roll out the dough until large enough to line the base and sides of the tin. Line the tin with the pastry and refrigerate for at least 1 hour. Preheat the oven to 190°C/375°F/gas mark 5.

Line the pastry case with a sheet of baking parchment and fill with baking beans or uncooked rice. Bake blind for 10 minutes, then remove the beans and baking parchment and bake for a further 5 minutes.

While the case is baking, make the filling. Melt the butter and syrup together in a saucepan. In a bowl, whisk the eggs and sugar together until light and fluffy. Add the melted butter mixture and mix well, then stir in the chopped pecans. Spread the filling into the pastry case and bake until set, about 25 minutes. Serve warm with ice-cold whipped cream or ice cream.

BAKED RHUBARB AND STRAWBERRIES WITH ICE CREAM AND TOASTED FLAKES

During the winter I always keep strawberries and rhubarb in my freezer, saved from the summer. So when the longing for warm summer days becomes too overwhelming I prepare this dessert, and remind myself how much I appreciate the four seasons. You will need to start making the vanilla ice cream the day before. In summer, use fresh rhubarb and strawberries rather than frozen and cook for 5 minutes less.

SERVES 6

For the vanilla ice cream
1 vanilla pod (bean)
500ml/2 cups single
   (light) cream
6 egg yolks
75g/scant ½ cup caster
   (granulated) sugar

For the toasted flakes
20g/¾oz rye flakes
20g/¾oz spelt flakes
20g/¾oz jumbo oats

For the baked fruit
1 vanilla pod (bean)
300g/10½oz frozen rhubarb
   slices
300g/10½oz frozen
   strawberries
75g/scant ½ cup caster
   (granulated) sugar

Start by making the ice cream the day before. Split the vanilla pod (bean) in half lengthways and scrape out the seeds using the tip of a knife. Put the cream, vanilla seeds and pod into a pan and bring to the boil, then remove from the heat. Meanwhile, whisk the egg yolks and sugar together in a large bowl until pale and fluffy. Gradually whisk in the hot cream mixture, then pour back into the pan again and heat slowly, stirring, until it starts to thicken. Leave to cool, then chill. Pour the mixture into a freezer-proof container and freeze for about 2–3 hours, taking it out now and then to give it a good stir, until the ice cream is frozen and set. (Alternatively, churn in an ice-cream machine.)

The next day, preheat the oven to 180°C/350°F/gas mark 4.

Mix the flakes and oats together and spread out on a baking sheet lined with baking parchment. Bake for 5 minutes.

For the baked fruit, split the vanilla pod in half lengthways and scrape out the seeds with the tip of a knife. Put the frozen rhubarb and strawberries into a bowl and mix in the sugar and vanilla seeds. Divide the fruit between 6 ramekin dishes and bake in the oven for 10 minutes. Leave to rest for 5 minutes, then place 2 scoops of ice cream on each, sprinkle with toasted flakes and serve right away.

WALNUT KISSES

In Danish we call a small meringue a kiss, or *kys*, because they are as delightful as one. Sweet, crunchy and melting like air in the mouth.

MAKES 40

4 egg whites
250g/1¼ cups caster
  (superfine) sugar
½ tsp vinegar
150g/5¼oz walnuts,
  chopped

Preheat the oven (not fan) to 110°C/225°F/gas mark ¼. Line 2 baking sheets with baking parchment.

Using an electric hand whisk, whisk the egg whites until stiff, then whisk in the sugar 1 tbsp at a time, until very stiff and all the sugar has been added. Add the vinegar and fold in the chopped walnuts.

Using 2 spoons, place dollops of the meringue mixture on the sheets (not too neat; they should look rustic). Bake for 1 hour, then turn off the heat, open the oven door and leave it ajar for 15 minutes. Take the meringues out of the oven and leave to cool completely on a wire rack, still on their sheets of baking parchment. Serve right away, or pack into cellophane bags and give away as gifts. They last for weeks in a cake tin. They are also great crushed over ice cream.

ICE CREAM CAKE

In summer, ice cream shops open everywhere in the city or at the beach, even getting mobile on ice cream bicycles on hot summer days. Everybody seems to love ice cream here, and it's not unusual to see long queues in front of an ice cream shop. The best shops make their own cones on the spot; served like this it's called an old-fashioned ice cream. In many shops you can order an ice cream cake for special occasions, or you can make your own. You need to make this the day before so it can freeze and settle before being served. It can be made days ahead if necessary.

SERVES 8–10

For the ice cream
1 litre/4 cups plus 3 Tbsp
   double (heavy) or single
   (light) cream
12 egg yolks
150g/generous ¾ cup caster
   (superfine) sugar

For the sponge
Butter, for greasing
4 eggs
120g/⅔ cup caster
   (superfine) sugar
30g/⅓ cup cocoa powder
Pinch of salt

For the caramel
200g/generous 1 cup caster
   (superfine) sugar

For decoration
100g/3½oz dark chocolate
   (60% cocoa solids), melted

For the sponge, preheat the oven to 180°C/350°F/gas mark 4. Line a round 28-cm/11-in springform cake tin with baking parchment and butter the baking parchment.

Separate the eggs and whisk the whites until stiff, then whisk in half the sugar a little at a time until you have used all the sugar and the mixture is a shiny, stiff meringue. Whisk the egg yolks in a separate bowl with the remaining sugar until fluffy and pale, then sift in the cocoa powder and salt. Fold the beaten egg whites into the egg yolk mixture and spread it evenly into the tin. Bake for 10 minutes. Leave to cool in the tin.

For the caramel, add the sugar to a dry pan and let it melt gently over a medium heat; do not stir, just shake the pan gently now and then. When it has turned golden (don't let it go too dark or it will taste bitter), pour onto a piece of baking parchment and leave to cool and harden.

For the ice cream, put the cream into a pan and bring to the boil, then remove from the heat. Meanwhile, whisk the egg yolks and sugar together in a large bowl until pale and fluffy. Gradually whisk in the hot cream mixture, then pour back into the pan again and heat slowly, stirring, until it starts to thicken. Leave to cool, then chill. Crush the hard caramel and stir into the chilled mixture. Pour it into a freezer-proof container and freeze for about 2–3 hours, taking it out now and then to give it a good stir, until the ice cream is almost frozen. (Alternatively, churn in an ice-cream machine.) Now spoon it over the baked sponge and spread it evenly. Freeze for 2–3 hours.

Just before serving, dip a spoon into the melted chocolate and throw it at the cake from different angles until you have a wild decoration! Try not to decorate your kitchen at the same time. Serve right away.

HOT CHOCOLATE AND SWEET BUNS

This is the quintessential *hygge* moment. Go for a long brisk walk in the woods in the autumn, with the wind in the trees and in your face, then return home to a warm house and enjoy home-baked buns and hot chocolate.

MAKES 20 BUNS

For the buns

50g/1¾ oz fresh yeast
400ml/1½ cups plus 2 Tbsp
  lukewarm whole milk
100g/7 Tbsp soft butter
1 egg, lightly beaten,
  plus an extra beaten egg
  for brushing
600g/4½ cups strong white
  bread flour, plus extra for
  dusting
1 Tbsp caster (granulated)
  sugar
10g/⅓oz sea salt
2 tsp ground cardamom
100/3½oz raisins
100g/3½oz dried cranberries
100g/3½oz hazelnuts,
  medium chopped

For the hot chocolate

350g/¾lb good-quality dark
  chocolate (at least 60%
  cocoa solids), broken into
  pieces
2 litres/8½ cups whole milk
1–2 Tbsp caster (granulated)
  sugar, to taste
200ml/¾ cup double (heavy)
  cream, whipped, to serve

Crumble the yeast into the milk in a large mixing bowl, stir to dissolve, then mix in the butter and egg. Mix the flour, sugar, salt, cardamom, dried fruits and nuts together, add to the milk mixture and give it a good stir with a wooden spoon to mix. Knead the dough lightly on a floured surface, then replace in the bowl, cover with cling film and leave to rise for 2 hours.

Knead the dough gently again on a floured surface and form it into 20 buns, then place the buns on baking sheets lined with baking parchment. Cover with tea towels and leave to rise for 30 minutes. Preheat the oven to 200°C/400°F/gas mark 6.

Brush the risen buns with beaten egg and bake in the oven for 20–25 minutes, then leave to cool on a wire rack.

For the hot chocolate, put the chocolate into a heavy-based saucepan and gently melt, stirring all the time, then add a quarter of the milk and stir it into the chocolate, followed by the remaining milk, mixing it well. Now stir in the sugar to taste, then bring the mixture to just under boiling point, stirring constantly so that it doesn't scorch. Take off the heat and pour into mugs. Add spoonfuls of cold whipped cream to the tops and serve with the freshly baked buns, and some butter.

WINTER APPLE LAYER CAKE

Danes have a special love for layer cakes, especially homemade ones; there are a lot of family recipes! These crisp layers are a classic Danish way to make the layer cake at home, and I always make this in winter. The cream for this is partly inspired by my favourite Danish author Karen Blixen – she has described the cake as part of her dinner party repertoire.

SERVES 8

For the apple sauce
600g/1lb 5oz Bramley apples
40g/¼ cup caster
 (granulated) sugar
1 Tbsp lemon juice

For the layers
175g/¾ cup minus 1 tsp
 soft butter
175g/¾ cup caster
 (granulated) sugar
1 egg
175g/1⅓ cups plain
 (all-purpose) flour
3 tsp ground cinnamon
2 tsp ground cardamom

For the cream
100g/3½oz hazelnuts
400ml/generous 1½ cups
 double (heavy) cream
100ml/scant ½ cup single
 (light) cream
2 tsp icing (confectioners')
 sugar

Peel and dice the apples and put them into a pan with the sugar and lemon juice. Let them simmer for 15–20 minutes until you have a smooth sauce. Set aside to cool.

Preheat the oven to 200°C/400°F/gas mark 6. Draw a 20-cm/8-in circle using a pencil on 7 sheets of baking parchment. Turn these over and arrange on as many baking sheets as necessary to fit (you may have to bake these in batches).

Beat the butter and sugar together until fluffy, then beat in the egg. Mix the flour and spices together and fold into the creamed mixture. Using a spatula, spread the mixture as evenly as possible inside each visible circle on the pieces of baking parchment.

Bake in the oven, in batches if necessary, for 6–8 minutes or until the edges start to take on some colour. Set aside to cool on the sheets of baking parchment on a wire rack.

While the layers are cooling, roast the hazelnuts. Spread them out on a baking sheet and roast in the oven, then wrap them in a clean tea towel and give them a good rub, so the skins come off. Roughly chop them.

Whip both creams together with the icing (confectioners') sugar and stir in two-thirds of the chopped hazelnuts.

Assemble the cake just before serving, and no sooner as it goes soft very quickly. Place a crisp layer on a serving plate and add some apple sauce, then add another crisp layer, then some cream. Repeat this layer pattern twice, then add the last crisp layer and some apple sauce on top. Sprinkle the remaining chopped hazelnuts on top and serve right away.

COFFEE BREAD

Coffee bread is so named because it used to be served in the informal coffee breaks that Danish people, especially women, took during the day. Today that would be at work, probably in an office, but 50 years ago it would have been in the kitchen with your neighbour, and would be part of women's daily culture during the week. It was very rude not to serve something with the coffee, and many of the sweet things we serve before lunch involve something made with bread. Using leftover bread is a long tradition going back to when Scandinavia was a poor region and food had much more value than it has today. We simply could not afford food waste. There are many ways to turn bread into sweet things, and this is one of them. If you do not have any leftover bread (any type can be used), make the one I have included here.

MAKES 40

For the bread
50g/3½ Tbsp soft butter
400g/3 cups strong white bread flour, plus extra for dusting
50g/⅓ cup caster (granulated) sugar
10g/⅓oz sea salt
25g/generous ¾oz fresh yeast
250ml/1 cup water

For the marzipan mixture
200g/7oz marzipan
300g/1⅔ cups caster (superfine) sugar
3–4 organic egg whites
50g/6 Tbsp plain (all-purpose) flour
½ tsp baking powder

Start by crumbling the butter into the flour in a mixing bowl, then stir in the sugar and salt. Dissolve the yeast in the water and add to the flour mixture, stirring to mix to a dough. Knead the dough well on a floured surface, return to the bowl, cover and leave to rise for 30 minutes.

Divide the dough in half and roll each half into a rectangle measuring about 12 x 34cm/4¾ x 13½in. Place both rectangles on a baking sheet lined with baking parchment and leave to rise for 1 hour. Preheat the oven to 180°C/350°F/gas mark 4.

Bake the bread for 20 minutes, then leave to cool on a wire rack. When cold, cut each rectangle into 20 slices and place on a wire rack with the cut side facing up. Toast in the oven until crisp, about 10 minutes.

While the bread slices are in the oven, grate the marzipan and mix with the sugar in a bowl. Add the egg whites a little at a time and whisk with a balloon whisk to a smooth mixture, then mix in the flour and baking powder. When the bread slices come out of the oven, spread the marzipan mixture onto each slice of bread, using a spoon or piping bag. Return to the oven and bake for 10–15 minutes or until golden brown. Leave to cool a little, then serve warm with a nice cup of coffee. Stored in an airtight container, they keep for a couple of weeks.

BUTTERMILK FROMAGE WITH GOOSEBERRY COMPOTE AND ALMOND MACAROONS

Despite its name, fromage is not cheese, but is more like panna cotta. The name comes from the Latin, where a case is called *forma*, which over time has changed into fromage – maybe because cheese is also made in a case. I love the light, creamy texture and fresh taste from the buttermilk. Buttermilk puddings are very much for warm and breezy summer days: hygge is not only for winter, but also for summer's bright nights.

SERVES 6

For the buttermilk fromage
4 sheets of leaf gelatine
   (2g per sheet)
1 vanilla pod (bean)
200ml/¾ cup double
   (heavy) cream
50g/scant ¼ cup caster
   (granulated) sugar
600ml/2½ cups buttermilk

For the gooseberry compote
400g/14oz gooseberries
130g/¾ cup caster
   (granulated) sugar

For the macaroons
2 egg whites
100g/generous ½ cup caster
   (superfine) sugar
100g/¾ cup whole almonds,
   finely ground in a food
   processor

This recipe is in 3 parts, and I always start with making the buttermilk fromage. Soak the gelatine in a little cold water until soft. Split the vanilla pod (bean) in half lengthways and scrape out the seeds with the tip of a knife. Place the cream, sugar and vanilla seeds in a pan and bring to the boil. Remove from the heat and set aside for 2 minutes. Lift the gelatine out of the water and squeeze out the water. Add the drained gelatine to the cream mixture and whisk well to distribute it evenly. Pour the mixture into a mixing bowl, add the buttermilk and gently mix.

Pour the tepid fromage mixture into a large serving bowl or 6 individual glasses, about 200ml/¾ cup each. Set aside until the fromage starts to set, then cover with cling film and refrigerate for at least 6 hours, or overnight.

For the gooseberry compote, place the gooseberries in a pan and let them simmer over a low heat for about 10 minutes, then add the sugar, stir well and simmer for another 15 minutes. Leave to cool, then store in jars in the fridge. It will not keep for more than 2–3 weeks.

Heat the oven (not fan) to 110°C/225°F/gas mark ¼. Line a baking sheet with baking parchment. Whisk the egg whites until they form stiff peaks, then add the sugar, 1 Tbsp at a time, whisking well after each addition, until all the sugar has been used and the mixture is smooth and shiny. Fold in the ground almonds. Use a teaspoon to spoon about 25 small mounds of the mixture onto the lined baking sheet, leaving a space between each.

Bake for about 50 minutes, then increase the oven temperature to 140°C/275°F/gas mark 1 and bake for about 10 minutes more or until golden. Carefully lift the baking parchment from the sheet, with the macaroons still on it, and transfer to a wire rack to cool. When ready to serve, spoon some compote on top of the fromage, crumble the macaroons and sprinkle over the compote. Serve right away.

ALMOND FRUIT CAKE

Dried fruit is one of those things you either love or hate. I belong to the group who loves all dried fruit, so for any cake or bread with dried fruit: count me in! This cake is perfect for afternoon tea in winter and autumn, but the truth is, I would eat it all year round.

SERVES 10–12

200g/1½ cups blanched
   almonds
200g/14 Tbsp soft butter,
   plus extra for greasing
250g/1¼ cups/8¾oz caster
   (granulated) sugar
4 eggs
150g/1 cup plus 2 Tbsp
   plain (all-purpose) flour
2 tsp baking powder
About 100ml/½ cup
   whole milk

For the dried fruit
100g/3½oz raisins
75g/2½oz candied lemon
   peel (ideally cedrat)
75g/2½oz candied orange
   peel
50g/6 Tbsp plain (all-purpose
   flour)

Preheat the oven to 180°C/350°F/gas mark 4. Butter a 26cm/10-in springform cake tin and line the base with baking parchment.

Start by folding the dried fruit through the flour and set aside for later.

Blitz the whole almonds to a paste in a food processor, adding a splash of water if necessary. Cream the butter and sugar together using an electric mixer, then add the almond paste and fold in until light and fluffy. Add the eggs one at a time, beating well after each addition.

Sift the flour and baking powder together and fold into the creamed mixture with a spatula, adding enough of the milk to reach a dropping consistency. Now fold in the flour-coated dried fruit.

Pour the batter into the prepared tin and bake in the oven for 1 hour, or until a skewer inserted into the centre comes out clean. Remove from the tin and leave to cool on a wire rack.

ROSENBRØD

Danish pastries, or *wienerbrød* as we call them, include a range of different small pieces of sweet pastry that we eat in the morning or before lunch. They are never savoury. These ones I used to love as a child, always looking out for them when I went to the bakery in the morning. Very few bakers still make them, but as the home-baked ones also taste so much better, I created my own recipe. I use my mother's homemade rose petal jelly from her garden for the icing; nothing can beat that!

MAKES 20–24

For the dough
25g/generous ¾oz fresh
   yeast
150ml/½ cup plus 2 Tbsp
   lukewarm water
1 egg, lightly beaten
1 tsp sea salt
½ tsp ground cardamom
1 Tbsp caster (granulated)
   sugar
325g/11½oz "00" flour,
   plus extra for dusting
300g/1⅓ cups cold butter,
   thinly sliced

For the glaze and icing
1 egg, beaten
8 Tbsp Rose Jelly (see page
   187 for homemade)
200g/scant 1½ cups icing
   (confectioners') sugar

Crumble the yeast into the water, stir to dissolve, then add the egg, salt, cardamom and sugar. Stir in the flour and knead the dough with your hands until it is even and combined. Put it in a bowl, cover with cling film and leave to rest in the fridge for about 15 minutes.

Roll out the dough on a lightly floured surface into roughly a 45-cm/18-in square. Arrange the butter slices in a square in the centre of the dough, at a 45-degree angle to the corners of the dough so it forms a smaller diamond inside the dough square. Fold the corners of the dough over the butter to encase it fully and seal the joins well. Roll out the dough again carefully, this time into a rectangle, making sure that it does not crack and expose the butter.

Fold a short end one-third over into the centre, and the other short end over that, as you would a business letter. Wrap in cling film and rest again in the fridge for 15 minutes. Repeat this rolling and folding procedure three times in total, remembering to let the dough rest for 15 minutes in the fridge between each.

Roll out the dough on a floured surface to a rectangle about 60 x 40cm/ 24 x 16in and divide in two. Now roll each out again and fold one half over the other half to make a rectangle, then place on 2 baking sheets lined with baking parchment and let it rise for 30 minutes.

Preheat the oven to 220°C/425°F/gas mark 7. Brush the dough with the beaten egg twice and then bake in the oven for 20 minutes. Leave to cool on a wire rack.

Now make the icing. Melt the rose petal jelly in a pan, add the icing (confectioners') sugar and whisk until smooth. Spread evenly on the rosenbrød and let it settle for 30 minutes. Now cut into 5-cm/2-in slices.

RAW BITES

It's a very interesting phenomenon these days that raw bars are regarded as this new thing in all the drive for vegan, gluten-free food. It will probably be no surprise to anyone to hear that I do not really buy into all these ideas about living by strange and arbitrary rules. Food for me is all about joy, history and culture. In the 1970s we ate a lot of weird things because it was the fashion in hippie culture. I experimented a lot with making candy bars with dried fruit and have loved raw bars for years.

MAKES 30

140g/5oz almonds, skin on
120g/4½oz raisins
275g/9½oz dates, stoned
50g/1¾oz coconut oil
50g/1¾oz cacao powder
50ml/scant ¼ cup freshly
   squeezed orange juice
½ tsp pure vanilla powder or
   natural vanilla extract
1 tsp ground cinnamon
100g/3½oz desiccated
   (shredded) coconut, to coat

Grind the almonds to a powder in a food processor.

Add all the ingredients except the coconut to a food processor and process to a smooth paste. Remove from the processor and form into small squares by hand. You should get about 30 bars. Roll in the desiccated (shredded) coconut to serve. They will keep in the refrigerator for 2–3 weeks.

POPPY SEED DANISH

If you go to a bakery in Denmark and ask for a snail, you will get a Danish with a swirl of cinnamon filling. I can't get enough of poppy seeds in any form of pastry, so I make poppy seed swirls instead. This is perfect in my world.

MAKES 18

For the dough

25g/generous ¾oz fresh yeast
150ml/½ cup plus 2 Tbsp lukewarm water
1 egg, lightly beaten, plus an extra beaten egg to glaze
1 tsp sea salt
½ tsp ground cardamom
1 tbsp caster (granulated) sugar
325g/11½ oz "00" flour, plus extra for dusting
300g/1⅓ cups cold butter, thinly sliced

For the filling

75g/5 Tbsp soft butter
75g/scant ½ cup caster (granulated) sugar
100g/3½oz raisins, chopped
75g/2½oz poppy seeds

Crumble the yeast into the water, stir to dissolve, then add the egg, salt, cardamom and sugar. Stir in the flour and knead the dough with your hands until it is even and combined. Put it in a bowl, cover with cling film and leave to rest in the fridge for about 15 minutes.

Roll out the dough on a lightly floured surface into roughly a 45-cm/18-in square. Arrange the butter slices in a square in the centre of the dough, at a 45-degree angle to the corners of the dough so it forms a smaller diamond inside the dough square. Fold the corners of the dough over the butter to encase it fully and seal the joins well. Roll out the dough again carefully, this time into a rectangle, making sure that it does not crack and expose the butter.

Fold a short end one-third over into the centre, and the other short end over that, as you would a business letter. Wrap in cling film and rest again in the fridge for 15 minutes. Repeat this rolling and folding procedure three times in total, remembering to let the dough rest for 15 minutes in the fridge between each.

Now make the filling. Mix the ingredients together until combined. Line 2 baking sheets with baking parchment.

Roll out the dough on a floured surface to a rectangle about 60 x 40cm/24 x 16in. Spread the filling evenly over the dough and, with the longest side facing you, roll it up like a Swiss roll. Cut the roll into 1.5-cm/½-in pieces and place, cut side up, on the lined baking sheets. Cover with tea towels and let them rise for 30 minutes. Preheat the oven to 220°C/425°F/gas mark 7.

Brush the snails with beaten egg and bake for 15–18 minutes.

MAZARIN CAKES

When I was a child, my siblings, cousins and I loved our grandmother's mazarin cake. It was a crazy green from the food colouring and probably tasted more artificial than I would appreciate today. I discussed recently with one of my cousins whether we should try making it again, and we agreed just to let that cake remain a happy memory. Here is the recipe for the mazarin cakes I bake today.

MAKES 24

250g/8¾oz marzipan, grated
250g/1¼ cups caster
    (superfine) sugar
250g/1 cup plus 2 Tbsp soft
    butter, plus extra
    for greasing
5 eggs
70g/½ cup plus ½ Tbsp plain
    (all-purpose) flour
Blueberries, raspberries,
    redcurrants and edible
    flowers, to decorate

For the frosting

1 vanilla pod (bean)
200ml/¾ cup plus 1 Tbsp
    full-fat crème fraîche
2 tbsp icing (confectioners')
    sugar

Preheat the oven to 190°C/375°F/gas mark 5.

Beat the grated marzipan with the sugar in a mixing bowl (you get the best result using an electric mixer), then add the butter and beat again until smooth. Add the eggs one at a time, beating between additions, until the mixture is even and smooth, then fold in the flour. Transfer the mixture to a piping bag and pipe into silicone mini-muffin moulds, about 3cm/1¼in in diameter (just use a spoon if you don't have a piping bag), filling the moulds to just below the rim. Now bake in the oven for 10 minutes then remove and leave to cool in the silicon moulds.

For the frosting, split the vanilla pod (bean) in half lengthways and scrape out the seeds using the tip of a knife. Put the crème fraîche in a mixing bowl, add the vanilla seeds and whisk until stiff, using an electric mixer or stand mixer. Stir in the icing (confectioners') sugar and transfer to a clean piping bag (if you have one, or you can use a spoon) and refrigerate until ready to use.

When the mazarins have cooled, take them out of the moulds, pipe a small dollop of frosting onto each, then decorate with the berries and edible flowers.

WAFFLES WITH RED GOOSEBERRY JAM AND CRÈME FRAÎCHE

As a child I spent most of every summer at my grandparents' beach house, which was part of a group of very small houses, lined up like a string of pearls next to each other and set back just yards from the sea. We more or less lived outdoors for the whole summer, with activities tailored to the weather. One thing we loved was to make a fire on the beach, and a dough that we put on sticks to cook over the fire. We also melted sugar in shells we found on the beach; we would set the shells aside so the sugar would turn to hard candy. It was such a treat, and real fun.

MAKES 12

1 vanilla pod (bean)
300g/2¼ cups plain (all-purpose) flour
2 tsp baking powder
1 Tbsp finely grated unwaxed lemon zest
½ tsp freshly grated nutmeg
3 Tbsp caster (superfine) sugar
1 tsp sea salt
4 eggs
500ml/2 cups plus 1 Tbsp buttermilk
100g/½ cup butter, melted, plus extra (salted) for cooking

To serve
Red Gooseberry "Jam" (see page 182)
Crème fraîche

Split the vanilla pod (bean) in half lengthways and scrape out the seeds using the tip of a knife. Mix the flour, baking powder, lemon zest, vanilla seeds, nutmeg, sugar and salt in a mixing bowl. Whisk in the eggs and buttermilk, using an electric mixer, then fold in the melted butter.

Heat up a cast-iron waffle mould (if cooking outside on the fire), add a little butter, then pour in the batter and cook over the open fire, turning the waffle iron until the waffle inside is crisp. Alternatively, you can do this inside over a gas hob, or use an electric waffle iron. Repeat with the remaining batter, and serve with the "jam" and some crème fraîche.

INDEX

ACKNOWLEDGMENTS

1000 TAK! Writing a cookbook is always teamwork, so there are a lot of people without whose hard work and support I could not have done this.

Thanks to Niels Peter Hahnemann for all your love every day. To my daughter Michala Hahnemann for love and an honest perspective. To my mother Hanne Rodam for love, support, and hard work on testing family recipes and sharing our family's food stories. To all my friends for eating joyfully at my dinner table for many, many years.

To my amazing agent Heather Holden-Brown for love and support and lots of fun. To Kelly Conway for taking part and eating with joy. To Allan Jenkins for believing in me and for all your support over the years.

To my super assistant Anne Sofie Rørth: without you I would never be able to produce a book; you are outstanding. To Columbus Leth: thank you for being so easy and professional at the same time. You make my stories and food come to life.

To the team at Quadrille: thank you to everybody, and a special thanks to Céline Hughes and Helen Lewis for being passionate, working hard on making my ideas come true, and understanding all my ideas and queries. To Sarah Lavelle for believing in me. To Arielle Gamble and Emily Lapworth for doing an amazing job designing the book. To Margaux Durigon and Hillary Farley for working endlessly to make my book sell. And to the rest of the team at Quadrille.

1000 TAK to the whole team at Hahnemanns Køkken – you inspire me every day. To head chefs Stig Jensen and Thomas Møller for recipe support, working with me in the kitchen, sharing my love for cooking, and backing me up when the pressure is on. To Shila Christensen for always inspiring new ways of cooking. To apprentice Mie Deurmann Petersen for giving your time and being so positive. To Sonja Bock for being right behind me and sharing your ideas generously.

Publishing director Sarah Lavelle
Creative director Helen Lewis
Commissioning editor Céline Hughes
Design concept Arielle Gamble
Designer Emily Lapworth
Production Emily Noto, Vincent Smith

First published in 2016 by Quadrille, an imprint of Hardie Grant Publishing

Quadrille
52–54 Southwark Street
London SE1 1UN
quadrille.com

Text © 2016 Trine Hahnemann
Photography © 2016 Columbus Leth
Design and layout © 2016 Quadrille Publishing

Cataloguing-in-Publication Data: a catalogue record for this book is available from the British Library.

Reprinted in 2016 (twice), 2017 (twice), 2018
10 9 8 7 6

UK ISBN: 978 1 84949 886 9
US ISBN: 978 1 84949 859 3

Printed in China